Legends of the North York Moors

Traditions . Beliefs . Folklore . Customs

by

Marion Atkinson

DALESMAN BOOKS
1981

The Dalesman Publishing Company Ltd.
Clapham, via Lancaster LA2 8EB

First published 1981

ISBN: 0 85206 623 6

'Men credit most easily the things which they do not understand. They believe most readily things which are obscure.'—Tacitus.

Dedicated to my good friend Glenys.

Printed in Great Britain by
GEORGE TODD & SON
Marlborough Street, Whitehaven

CONTENTS

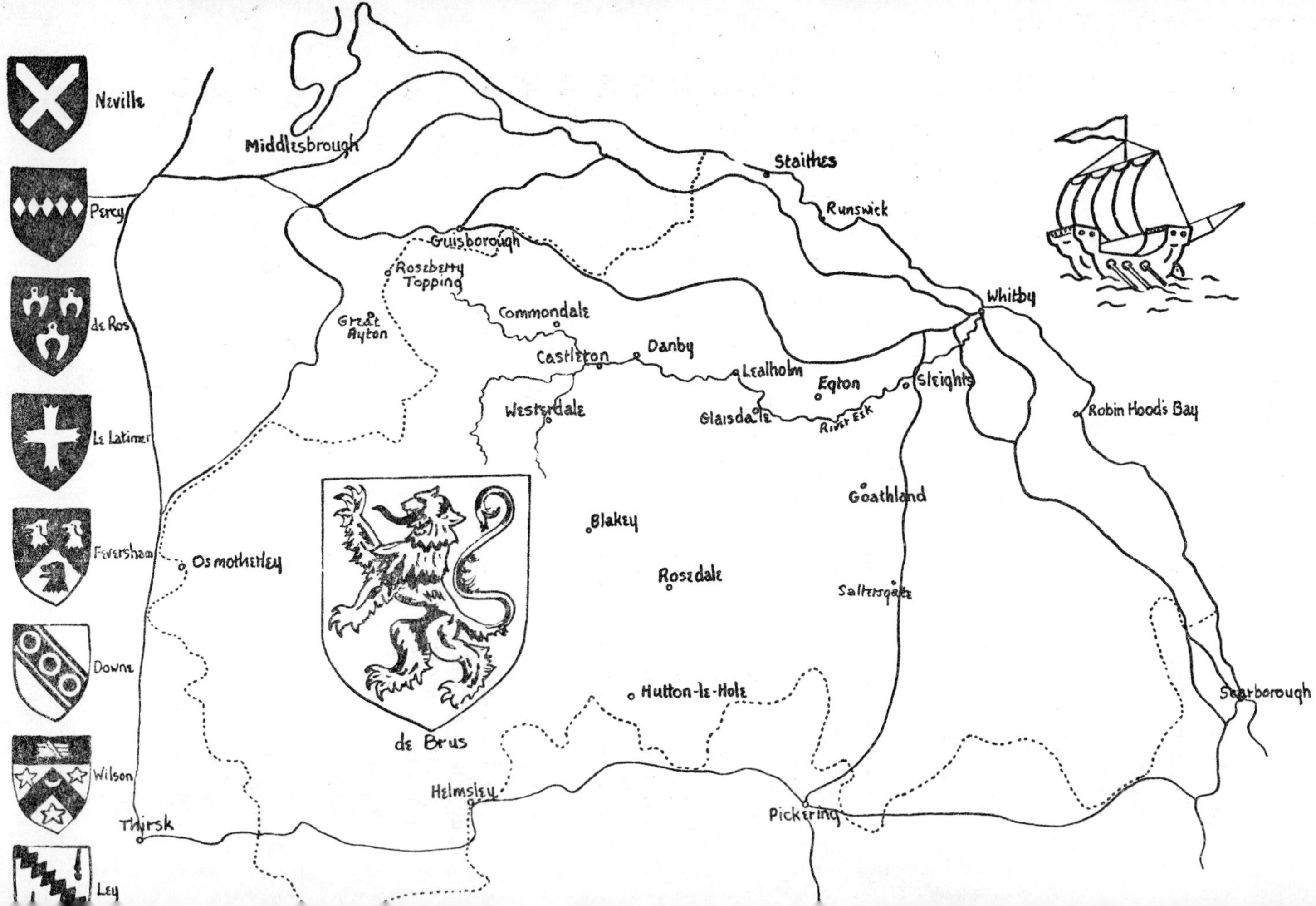

Neville
Percy
de Ros
le Latimer
Feversham
Downe
Wilson
Ley
Middlesbrough
Staithes
Runswick
Guisborough
Roseberry Topping
Great Ayton
Commondale
Castleton
Danby
Lealholm
Egton
Sleights
Whitby
Robin Hood's Bay
Westerdale
Glaisdale
River Esk
Goathland
Blakey
Osmotherley
Rosedale
Saltersgate
Hutton-le-Hole
Scarborough
de Brus
Helmsley
Pickering
Thirsk

INTRODUCTION

THE north-east of Yorkshire is an area of ancient memories. Ancient beliefs, legendary tales, folklore, and stories involving giants, hobs and fairies were formerly commonplace. Many of these stories can be traced back to the early inhabitants of this area—the Bronze Age peoples and the Celts. Fairies and hobs were implicitly believed in. Fairies, supposedly being the ever present spirits of the dead, give their name to various places, for example Fairy Cross Plain at Fryup where they are said to have been seen dancing around the fairy rings. Hobs, too, some malicious and some friendly, gave their own names to places, such as Hob of Hart Hall and Hob of Hasty Bank.

When we are confronted by so many awesome examples of information made possible by modern scientific technology, we can be forgiven for imagining that there is not much left to discover and that unsolved mysteries will soon be things of the past. Unsolved mysteries are very annoying to the human mind, and in the same way as a grain of sand irritates an oyster, so, man intrigued by mysteries he does not understand, creates a pearl around this irritation by inventing plausible reasons out of his imagination to explain events or happenings. Many of the traditional stories told are mere superstition and can simply be dismissed. But usually there is a grain of truth in most stories of folklore and legend.

Even today people believe in the existence of yetties; 'The Big Foot'; and the Loch Ness Monster, so therefore we should not believe that our forefathers were any more credulous than ourselves. Like us, they had fears and uncertainties and relied on their powers of imagination to explain what lay beyond the limits of their knowledge. But it is sceptical to say that all traditional stories must be so confused and embroidered by the passage of time that they contain no valid historical truth whatsoever.

Today there are many people who believe in the stars, ghosts, reincarnation, and the power of good luck charms. The person who touches wood for luck is echoing the custom of men long ago who revered the spirits of the trees. Throwing a coin into a wishing well for good fortune is based upon the pagan Celts who used to drop human heads into the water for the same reason. When you avoid walking under a ladder do you know why? Do you know that it goes back to the time when a condemned man had to climb a ladder to the gallows—the ladder then being twisted so that he fell to the rope's end beneath it. But for every superstition there is usually a traditional antidote. One of the most powerful being the horseshoe—a guardian that prevents entry by evil forces.

There are some beliefs which have stood the test of time, although they may not stand the test of reason. This book is about people and events in North East Yorkshire—traditional stories, beliefs and customs. Are they based on fact or fiction? A fact is defined as something, some object or condition that actually exists in space, or an event, mental or physical that has actually occurred; something which has been experienced. And fiction is defined as something that is imagined or invented. Perhaps the two combine traditionally and what we have are imagined stories embroidered on some elements of fact.

ACKNOWLEDGMENTS

Evening Gazette.
Ryedale Folk Museum.
Ruth Fletcher.
Michael Farthing.
Brian Krengel.
Forty Years in a Moorland Parish, J. C. Atkinson.
Witchcraft in Yorkshire, Patricia Crowther.
Yorkshire Legends, Dalesman.
Whitby Lore and Legend, Shaw Jeffrey.
Life in the Moorlands of N.E. Yorkshire, M. Hartley and J. Ingilby.
Tales of Haunting and Horror Around the North, Dane & MacNeal.
Some Reminiscences and Folklore of Danby Parish and District, Joseph Ford.
Goathland in History and Folklore, F. W. Dowson.
The Gytrash of Goathland and Other Yorkshire Legends, Michael Temple.
The Ballads and Songs of Yorkshire, Ingled.
The Father Postgate Story, Father David Quinlan.
Vampires, E. D. Baumann.
Yorkshire Village Life, Humour and Characters, J. Fairfax-Blakeborough.

The sketches are by the author.

THE PENNY HEDGE

Then Whitby's nuns exulting told
How to their house three barons bold
Must menial service do;
While horns blow out a note of shame,
And monks cry, 'Fye upon your name!
In wrath, for loss of sylvan game,
St. Hilda's priest ye slew
This on Ascension Day each year
Must Herbert, Bruce, and Percy hear.'

—From Scott's *Marmion.*

THIS unique custom of the planting of the Penny Hedge or Horngarth goes back a long way and is observed at Whitby every year—the morning of the eve of Ascension Day in a small inlet in the harbour. A hedge is constructed that will withstand a tide and a tide and a half. This hedge consists of bundles of stakes and osiers, cut with a knife of the value of 'one penny' and carried at sun-rise through the town to the harbour, on the backs of the men who are to build it. These stakes are planted at the water's edge near Green Lane at low tide—the 'yethers' (osiers) being woven through the 'stowers' (stakes) to form a 'hedge.' The name 'Penny Hedge' is probably a corruption of 'penance hedge.' The alternative name for this custom is 'Horngarth' and this word usually meant an enclosure for hunting, where certain tenants were obliged to build a horngarth so that the Lord of the Manor could round up the game and drive it into this. But whichever title this ritual is known by, both graphically portray and offer some explanation as to the contents of the legend. The story of Penny Hedge was originally taken from an ancient copy printed on vellum—the penance reads as follows:

'Then said the Hermit: "You and yours shall hold your Lands of the Abbot of Whitby, and his Successors in this manner: That upon Ascention Eve, you, or some of you, shall come to the Wood of the Strayhead, which is in Eskdale-Side, the same day at sun-rising, and there shall the Officer of the Abbot blow his horn, to the intent that you may know how to find him and he shall deliver unto you. William de Bruce, ten stakes, ten stout stowers and ten yedders, to be cut by you, or those that come for you, with a knife of a Penny Price; and you Ralph de Piercie, shall take one and twenty of each sort, to be cut in the same manner; and you Allatson, shall take nine of each sort, to be cut as aforesaid: and to be taken on your back, and carried to the town of Whitby, and so to be there before nine of the Clock" . . .'

This annual ritual always attracts many spectators although not all who watch know of its significance, but legend assigns its origin

to a strange happening in the Whitby district in the reign of Henry II. At this time Whitby Abbey was one of the most famous and powerful religious houses in the land being sanctified by the memory of St. Hilda; and it was here that the great Synod was held which united the ancient British Church with the Mission of Augustine. The Abbot of Whitby was therefore one of the most powerful and influential men at the time and it was considered foolish to anger him unnecessarily.

It was at this time that three local barons were out hunting wild boar in the area of Eskdale-side. They were of noble blood and held land, bestowed upon them by favour of successive Norman kings. They were William de Brus, Ralph de Percy and another known as Allatson. While they were out pursuing the sport of noblemen, they happened upon a fine wild boar. This animal provided great sport for them and gave them a good run—reinforcing their determination to kill it at all costs. The tired boar sought refuge where it could—the place it chose being the dwelling of the Hermit of Eskdale-side. The three barons and their retinue followed the animal and were exceedingly annoyed at the stubbornness of the holy man in his refusal to hand over the wounded and tired boar. But the frail old man was adamant that the boar was one of God's creatures and was to be shown mercy and protection in his sanctuary.

The barons were equally determined not to lose their quarry simply because of one old man. They were still inflamed by the excitement of the chase and ignoring his protests, they beat the old man to the ground and killed the animal (as tradition would have it) beneath the altar itself. When their excitement had abated at the sight of the dead animal lying in a pool of blood, they noticed that the hermit, whom they had brutally cast aside, did not stir, and was in fact dying from the injuries received at their hands. Then they realised what they had done, and the wrath they would incur from the abbot if this was discovered. But, as tends to be customary from such religious persons, the hermit forgave them before he died, making them promise in front of witnesses to carry out a penance. By forgiving them in such a public manner the holy man made it quite clear that this was no accident but murder, and that he had a great deal to forgive, and his death was to have satisfaction. They were so frightened that, ironically they sought refuge themselves—taking sanctuary at Scarborough.

On the discovery of their crime, the Abbot of Whitby decided to show mercy. He did not impose the maximum penalty against them, but instead their sentence was that they should surrender all their lands at Whitby Abbey, and that they and their heirs for ever should hold them of the Abbey by the tenure of the Penny Hedge. This tenure was obviously devised to belittle the noblemen and make them look as ridiculous as possible, by obliging them to carry bundles of hedge stakes upon their backs through the streets of the town in full view of everyone—in order to build a hedge by the water's side, accompanied by jeering crowds and the official blowing of a horn to announce their proceedings, crying 'Out upon you! Out upon you, for your grievous fault!'

CAEDMON

CAEDMON was a humble cowherd at the Abbey in the late seventh century, and his greatest desire was to be able to sing in tune so that he could join in the evening entertainment among his fellow workers. But Caedmon was stone deaf and could not therefore join in the singing without annoying his friends by making ridiculous noises, so he would retire to his bed early and unhappy. He prayed long and hard that he might be cured of his defect—this was not granted to him, but instead he had a vision of an angel who asked him to sing of the creation of the world. Bede tells of how, 'a person appeared to him in his sleep and saluting him by name, said, "Caedmon sing some song for me." He answered, "I cannot sing, for that was the reason why I left the gebeorscip (the evening entertainment), and retired to this place, because I could not sing." . . . "What shall I sing?" rejoined he. "Sing the beginning of created things," said the other. Hereupon he presently began to sing to the praise of God, verses which he had never heard:

Now must we praise the Warden of Heaven's realm,
The Creator's might and his mind's thought,
The glorious works of the Father, laid the foundation.
He shaped erst, for the sons of men.
Heaven as their roof, Holy Creator.
The middle world, He, mankind's Warden,
Eternal Lord, afterwards prepared,
The earth for men, Lord Almighty.'

On waking he sang his newly inspired hymn to the Abbess Hilda, who was most impressed by him. She ordered the learned monks to explain to Caedmon other passages of Scripture and he put these also successfully into the new style—of pagan Anglo-Saxon verse. The lines were short and alliterative as an aid to the memory, so that they could be sung like the old Viking war songs after a feast when the drinking horn was circulated round the assembly, and the harps also so that each man could sing (this was similar to the evening sing-song from which Caedmon was originally excluded).

Caedmon received the glory of having written the first poem ever couched in the English tongue, and the fact that this great profusion of English verse should first have been created in Whitby Abbey makes it a sacred spot indeed. One of Caedmon's manuscripts can be found in Cambridge University Library.

There is a memorial to Caedmon at the top of the Church Stairs in the parish churchyard. This cross stands twenty feet high and was hewn out of fine-grained sandstone from Northumberland. It was unveiled in 1898 to display panels depicting various religious and holy scenes. On the front are carved panels showing Christ in the act of blessing; David playing his harp; the Abbess Hilda; and Caedmon being inspired to sing his song in the Abbey stable. On the arms of the cross above, are the symbols of the four evangelists with the Agnus Dei in the middle. Below is the inscription:

TO THE GLORY
OF GOD AND IN
MEMORY OF
CAEDMON
THE FATHER
OF ENGLISH
SACRED SONG
FELL ASLEEP
HARD BY 680.

On the obverse side is carved a double vine, symbolic of Christ, and in the loops, figures of the four great scholars trained at Whitby

Abbey in Caedmon's time: Aetla, Oftfor, Bosa and John. Beneath this are the lines of Caedmon's hymn of the Creation. On the south side carved on the border of the English rose pattern is the Anglo-Saxon version of the hymn, and on the opposite side it is in Anglo-Saxon runes (an alphabet of straight lines used for carving inscriptions in Caedmon's time). These runes edge the north side which depicts an apple tree emblematic of the Garden of Eden.

ST. HILDA OF WHITBY ABBEY

SIR Walter Scott was so inspired by the legends of St. Hilda as to compose his poem *Marmion* on that theme. The fame of Whitby Abbey goes back to Anglo-Saxon times. Although it was founded and endowed by Osway, King of the Northumbrians, and was dedicated to St. Peter, the monastery was always ascribed to St. Hilda, who was so profoundly respected that a great many miracles were attributed to her wonderful powers. St. Hilda made such an impression on the people because of her devotion to the Abbey that it was believed that she never actually left her beloved monastery, but still wanders the grounds. A Whitby historian in 1776 mentioned this story, 'At a particular time of the year, viz. in the summer months, the sunbeams fall in the inside of the northern part of the choir, and 'tis then that the spectators who stand on the west side of Whitby churchyard, so as just to see the most northerly part of the abbey, past the north of Whitby church, imagine they perceive in one of the highest windows there the resemblance of a woman arranged in a shroud. Though we are certain this is only a reflection caused by the splendour of the sunbeams, yet report says, and it is constantly believed among the vulgar, to be an appearance of Lady Hilda, in her shroud or rather in her glorified state.'

Another legend relates how the Abbess St. Hilda rid Eskdale of snakes. When she founded the abbey it naturally became a sanctuary for many a hunted fugitive. But the abbey, built on such a conspicuous site not only attracted human fugitives it seems. There appears to have been an overabundance of unwelcomed guests to the monastery as well, in the form of snakes. Not just the odd one, but a veritable epidemic which was destroying the calm and dignity of some of the auspicious monastic activities. Complaints were received by the Abbess concerning the conditions and she obviously had to do something constructive to rid herself and the inmates of these tiresome and troublesome vipers. She did it by cursing the vipers, undoubtedly in Latin, and it appears to have worked because the poor demented snakes were driven to the edge of the cliff under the barrage of verbal abuse. But it seems that they were not very willing to throw themselves over, and when they reached the edge they turned round putting out their tongues and hissing at St. Hilda. This annoyed the good lady very much and under the influence of this sudden irritation she lashed out with her whip and decapitated them, sending the writhing headless bodies hurtling over the cliff onto the Scar below, where they all immediately turned into stone.

They can be found today on the Scar when the tide is out, as visible and tangible proof of the legend. Although there are those unbelieving persons among the general public who seek to find an alternative explanation to the headless stone snakes—they call them ammonites.

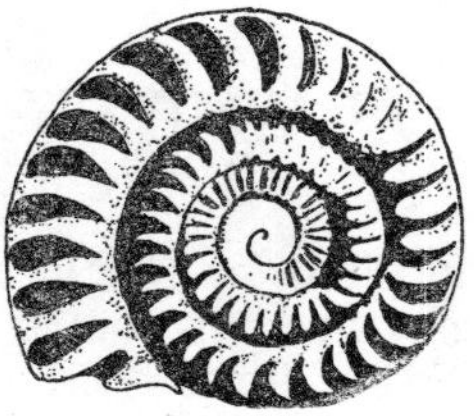

THE LEGEND OF THE BURIED CHIMES

AT the time of the Dissolution of the monasteries in 1539 all the valuable articles from the abbey were removed and either destroyed or sold. One of the articles that had been sold was an entire ring of bells. These bells were removed from the abbey and were to be taken by ship to London, but they were fated never to reach their destination, or in fact to leave Whitby. Although the sea was perfectly calm the ship never left the harbour. It slowly sank beneath the waters. This was seen as an act of Providence—by not allowing so flagrant a theft of Church property. The real reason was probably because of the extreme weight of the bells. These bells remain there under the water off the end of Black Nab and it is said that on a quiet night the sea fairies ring the bells and they can be heard by anyone who believes, and whose ears are not deaf to their tune.

Another version of this story mentions that the bells were actually being brought to the abbey and not being removed, in the following poem:

The Buried Chimes

by S. K. Phillips

Under the cliffs at Whitby, when the great tides landward flow,
Under the cliffs at Whitby, when the great winds landward blow,
When long billows heavily roll o'er the harbour bar,
And the blue waves flash to silver 'mid the seaweeds on the Scar,
When the low thunder of the surf calls down the hollow shore,
And 'mid the caves of Kettleness the baffled breakers roar.

Under the cliffs at Whitby, who so will stand alone
Where, in the shadow of the Nab, the eddies swirl and moan,
When, to the pulses of the deep, the flood-tide rising swells,
Will hear, amid its monotone, the clash of hidden bells.

Up from the heart of ocean the mellow music peals,
Where the sunlight makes its golden path, and the seamew flits and wheels,
For many a chequered century, untiring by flying time,
The bells, no human fingers touch, have rung their hidden chime,
Since the gallant ship that brought them, for the abbey on the height,
Struck and foundered in the offing, with her sacred goal in sight.

And the man who dares on Hallowe'en on the Black Nab to watch,
Till the rose-light on St. Hilda's shrine the midnight moonbeams catch,
And calls his sweet-heart by her name, as, o'er the sleeping seas,
The echo of the buried bells comes floating on the breeze,
'Ere another moon on Hallowe'en her eerie rays has shed,
Will hear his wedding peal ring out from the church tower on the Head.

DRACULA

BY the late eighteenth century when Gothic romances became popular, the vampire was an ideal character for stories set in mist-shrouded castles in faraway countries. In the early 1800s, the vampire made its first appearance on the stage. Writers such as Alexander Dumas churned out blood-curling plays about the exploits of these creatures. But it was not until 1897 that Bram Stoker, a relatively unknown Irish writer, launched his classic story *Dracula* upon the world.

Bram Stoker apparently based his character Count Dracula on Vlad The Impaler, a medieval tyrant of Wallachia, who took great delight in impaling his enemies alive. Vlad was known as Draculaea, son of the Devil. Vlad ruled this part of Rumania from 1456–1462, and in those six years he managed to execute 40,000 people—using the same gory methods (by impaling them on long stakes). There was no one who was exempt from his mad fantasies: prisoners of war, noble hangers-on in his own court, even priests and holy men who were usually revered. His strange whims also extended to visiting diplomats. On one occasion he nailed the slipper of the Turkish Ambassador to his skull and sent him back to Constantinople in a litter. He did this to express his contempt for all Turks, diplomatically of course!

Bram Stoker never visited Transylvania, but researched the material for his novels in the British Museum. He knew of the vampire legends

Dracula — Vlad the Impaler.

and knew that to kill an 'undead' body, a wooden stake had to be driven through its heart, echoing Vlad's habit of getting rid of unwanted guests. Stoker may have been further inspired by another bloody noble — the Hungarian countess Elizabeth Bathory. She was the wife of General Ferencz Nadasdy, and lived in a castle deep in the dark Carpathian mountains. Whenever her husband was away (and he was often away on various military campaigns), the beautiful neglected countess relieved her boredom by gathering around her a sinister band of witches and sorcerers who indulged her in the belief that drinking and bathing in the blood of young girls would preserve her beauty. And so, at the dead of night, the countess and her dedicated band of followers would travel around the countryside in a black coach hunting for girls. Any that they found were kidnapped and driven back to the castle. Here in the castle the young girls were brutally tortured and then hung up on chains like carcasses of beef while their blood was drained to fill the countess's bath.

Rumours of her wicked deeds travelled far and wide and finally reached the ears of Hungarian king Matthias II. He ordered his men to search the castle and they found the bodies of many young girls still hanging from chains in the dungeons. At her trial, the countess was convicted of murdering some sixty girls. Her retinue and accomplices in her reign of terror were beheaded or burnt at the stake. But Countess Elizabeth Bathory herself escaped execution because of her noble birth. Instead she was condemned to a living death—walled up in a tiny room in her own castle. She was kept alive in her tomb by scraps of food being pushed through a small slit, and four years later, still in her tomb, she died.

In one of Stoker's short stories a man travelling to Castle Dracula seeking shelter from a storm in a cemetery finds the tomb of a noblewoman—with an iron stake driven into her coffin echoing the fate of the countess. Like many stories that have been absorbed into folklore, the vampire legend has some medically factual backing. Interbreeding among eastern European nobility during the late Middle Ages led to various genetic disorders, including a rare disease known as 'Erythropoietic Protoporphyria.' Although this particular disease was not diagnosed until the nineteenth century, records of the time have convinced doctors that many so-called vampires were in fact victims of this disease, which makes the body produce too much porphyrin—a substance that is the basis of red blood cells. This results in redness of the skin, eyes and teeth, a receding of the upper lip, and cracks in the skin which bleed when exposed to light. The only treatment known at the time for the condition was to lock the patients away during the day so that they were not exposed to daylight, and by encouraging them to drink blood to replace the amount they lost by bleeding. But rumours being what they are often get a little out of hand and knowledge of these nocturnal blood-drinkers could have led to a spate of vampire stories in the region—and encouraged Stoker to set Castle Dracula in the strange Eastern European land of Transylvania. But part of the background to the story is a little nearer home than Transylvania. Bram Stoker in fact chose Whitby as the background to *Dracula*, as it was in Whitby that the vampire Count Dracula came ashore in the shape of an 'immense dog' from the wreck of the 'Dementer August 8'; Whitby is also easily recognisable in the references to the conversations with Swales in the churchyard; by the description of the Russian schooner driven into the harbour by the storm and the spectral hound which was believed to haunt Haggerlythe (the old name for Henrietta Street).

BAGDALE OLD HALL

THE Conyers family were the most important people in the Whitby district and they were responsible for the building of Bagdale Hall as one of their residences at the beginning of the sixteenth century, in the days when it was surrounded by grass and a stream murmured gently nearby. It has changed hands many times since in the last four centuries and no doubt it has witnessed many strange happenings and incidents—this probably accounts for the Old Hall having acquired rather a sinister reputation. Owners were warned that they would find difficulty in persuading local servants to live in the Hall because of the sinister happenings—Bagdale Old Hall was haunted, the ghost manifesting itself in various ways. This ghost was apparently a poltergeist who seemed to enjoy throwing objects around the room. Loud crashes would be heard from time to time. These noises were said to come from inside the china cabinet in the kitchen, but even after the cupboard was removed, the noises were still heard and the actual china contents from the cabinet were still intact. As well as the loud crashing noises, footsteps were also heard on the creaking stairs of the central staircase. Guests staying at the old manor house often enquired as to the noise, thinking that they had heard people moving about during the night. Alterations were made and the builders secured any loose boards and wedged all the stair treads, but even today odd unaccounted for footsteps can still be heard on the stairs and in the hall, and even the inexplicable sound of bells ringing out can be heard every now and again.

The maid of a previous owner reported that she heard a noise while making a bed and when she turned round, she saw a figure in period costume. When she went back to making the bed two sheets were missing—and to this very day they have still remained missing. The maid was convinced that she had seen the ghost of a former occupant of Bagdale Old Hall, a Captain Browne Bushell. The Bushells were an old established Whitby family of master mariners, merchants and ship owners. Browne was born in 1609 and he grew up at the Hall. He married the daughter of Sir Thomas Fairfax, Cromwell's chief of staff and they lived at the Hall. Their happiness was to be short lived because the Captain became involved in the Civil War. He was in command of Scarborough Castle which surrendered to the Royalists. He was unable to make his mind up which of the two sides to support and so he played one off against the other. Eventually he was caught and imprisoned and it was three years before he was brought to trial, condemned and executed. Because of this it is said that the ghost at Bagdale Old Hall is the headless ghost of the Captain.

WITCHCRAFT

IT is only about a hundred years ago that people living in the north east of Yorkshire were great believers in magic and perhaps nowhere was the belief more common than in the Whitby area. The great fear and gullibility which had grown up in this area was the result of the superstitions built up over the centuries. Goathland still remembers Nancy Pierson who was able to turn herself into a hare, and Ruswarp had Old Kathy. In fact almost every village had its old woman who was supposedly capable of riding around on a broomstick, and changing herself into any shape or form she chose. These old ladies were the ones who were supposed to have brought sickness and bad luck to the household, and who cast the 'evil-eye.'

There were many ways of counteracting the influence of these evil spirits which were practised by the farmers. Hazel twigs were collected and made up into the form of a cross to be tied around the neck of cattle to prevent them from being bewitched; horseshoes were nailed over the stable doors for the same reason. Corn dollies, in the shape of birds, were stuck in the top of hay ricks to keep the witches away from them, because it was believed that the witch would become so engrossed in playing with these corn dollies that she would completely forget about casting evil spells upon the household. People went to strange lengths to avoid the danger of being bewitched, as Joseph Ford recalls in his *Some Reminiscences and Folklore of Danby Parish and District*. He knew a lady from Fryup who had a great dread of the powers of witchcraft, and when she was churning the butter she would place a sprinkling of salt into the butterchurn and at the same time she would take three steps backwards and throw a portion of the salt over her head into the fire. This was supposedly to protect her butter from any evil influences. People also carried good luck charms around with them, of which jet was a great favourite.

A 17th century charm to avert witch evil and illness.

Some examples of love charms to be found at the Ryedale Folk Museum. These charms were made of lead and sold by the witches to give safety in travel and to aid in love matters.

For centuries in the Whitby area jet amulets have been carried as a protective charm against evil. Craftsmen in and around Whitby have made these jet ornaments since the Bronze Age. In the nineteenth century jet became very fashionable when Queen Victoria went into mourning for Prince Albert. There were seven shops operating in Whitby then and many people were employed in the industry. Traditionally jet has had many uses in practical medicine and was prescribed for various complaints. During the Middle Ages it was known as Black Amber or Witches Amber, and like amber it was ground into a powder and burnt—the fumes were believed to repel plague germs, pestilence and fever. It was also used as a general fumigant. Some old Whitby wives used to scatter powdered jet upon the fires to ensure that their husbands would return safely from the sea. Jet was also supposed to have the power to cure dropsy and epilepsy, and to ease the pains of childbirth. It is still believed by some people that it will dispel depression and fear, as well as acting as a protection against thunder and lightning.

The very fact that people believed in witches and witchcraft made them very susceptible to laying the blame for any hardship onto some poor and innocent victim. As John Gaunt, vicar of Great Straughton wrote, 'Every old woman with a wrinkled face, a furred brow, a hairy lip, a gobber tooth, a squint eye, a squeaking voice, or a scolding tongue, having a rugged coat on her back, a skull-cap on her head, a spindle in her hand, and a dog or cat by her side, is not only suspected but pronounced a witch.'

Betty Strother, who lived near Castleton was said to be a sorceress, although she only practised white magic. Many men and women visited her in order to purchase her cures and good luck charms—not only for themselves but for their livestock. She was said to have possessed great powers in healing right up until her death in 1775. She had inherited a great deal of knowledge and skill from her mother, and amongst her regalia she possessed a magic looking glass, a crystal ball, magic cubes and a witch's garter. People came from far and near to consult her about their horoscopes as she was well versed in casting charts from the astrological tables. Amongst the stories of her powers is the following: she was once asked to purify a butter

A Witchs familiar – taken from a pamphlet in 1579

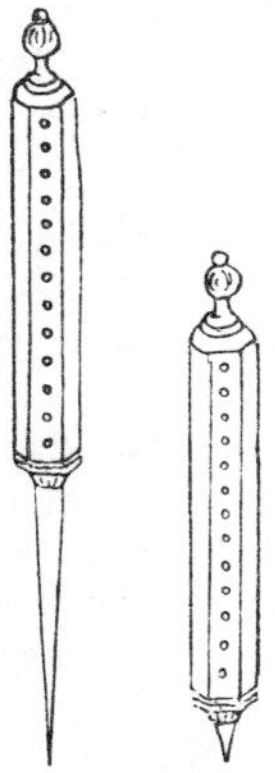

A witch pricker - having a retractable blade and a hollow shaft

Matthew Hopkins (Witch finder General)

churn supposedly cursed by the Devil. When the powder she gave was thrown into the churn, a serpent which turned into the Devil himself came out and made off. One of the most famous of local witches was Nanny Peirson from Goathland. She was accused of casting the evil-eye and bewitching both animals and humans. One story says how Nanny was seen to go into a china cupboard by making herself grow very small. She walked around inside this cupboard full of china pots without breaking a single piece.

Another old witch story relates what happened at an old house connected with the Bleach Mill at Commondale. At this old Bleach Mill a witch was supposed to have been causing a great deal of havoc and distress to the owner of the mill by casting her wicked spells on his cattle. Despite the fear and dread in which she was held, plans were made to carry out an elaborate scheme to counteract her evil spells. This plan involved the removal of the heart of one of the animals that was supposed to have died under the spell of this witch. Further preparation of this heart involved piercing it with nine new pins and an equal number of new needles and new nails. All of these were embedded in the heart which was to be burnt over a slow fire made of elder or rowan wood. Great care was taken to ensure that all the doors were barred and bolted and the windows were covered with heavy material to make certain that no light could be seen from the outside. This gruesome object was hung from a rannel hook and slowly allowed to frizzle over the fire, while those taking part in the proceedings watched the heart slowly shrivelling as the midnight hour drew near. The shrivelling of this burnt and blackened heart had to be manipulated very carefully to ensure that it burst into flames and fell to ashes as the clock struck twelve. At this crucial hour the leader of the proceedings began the final act by reading aloud two verses of a particular Psalm from the Scriptures. This story relates to spells and also the charms to remove them, which were resorted to under extenuating circumstances such as when the evil ways of the witch had reached such proportions that something drastic had to be done—and many and varied were the antidotes employed.

Witches were also endowed with the power to turn themselves into animals, usually into the form of a hare. And legend has it that there was once a plantation in Eskdale which was over-run with hares which were causing a great deal of damage. Many of these hares were shot, but there was one particular hare that was noted always to escape. After consulting a wise old man in the village on how they might rid themselves of this particular hare, the old man told them to shoot the hare with pieces of silver, as he believed that this hare was really an old woman from the village long suspected of being a witch. That same night they were determined to rid themselves of this hare once and for all. When they saw it, they took aim and fired, killing the hare. On their return a neighbour of the old lady rushed out of her cottage and told them that the old lady was dead. It appeared that at the very same moment the hare had been shot the 'witch' had thrown up her arms and screamed, 'They have killed my familiar spirit.'

Witch hunting became big business in the seventeenth century with people like Matthew Hopkins (The Witch-finder General). Experienced 'prickers' would be hired to discover the identity of witches. This was generally falsified by using a retractable blade because the searchers received more money the more people they pronounced as witches.

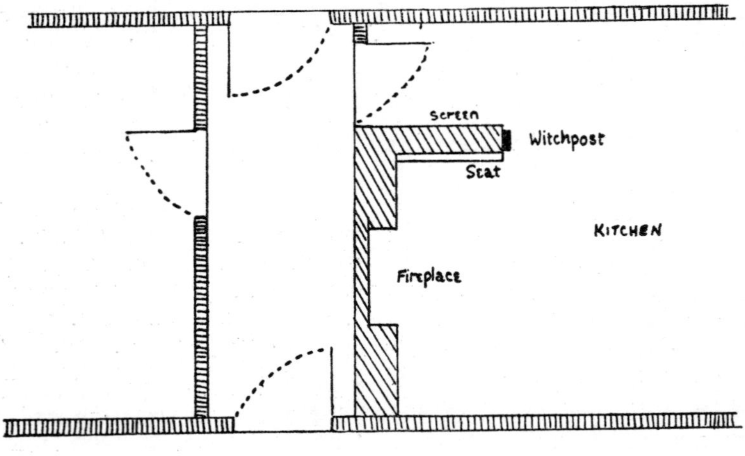

Above: Witch posts from (left to right) Stangend, Danby and Glaisdale. Opposite: Plan showing the usual position of the witch post.

One example of witch pricking in this part of Yorkshire happened in 1652 when Anne Hunnam of Scarborough was suspected of bewitching children, causing them to suffer from fits. She was searched for the Devil's mark and a small spot was found on her side. The pin was thrust into this mark. Because Anne did not move or appear to feel this 'prick' she was proclaimed as a witch. Anne probably did not feel any pain or need to flinch because a false pricker had been used. To the spectator it looked as though she had had a pin thrust into her side causing her no pain, and this proved that the Devil was protecting her.

A further protection from witches was the possession of a witch post in the house—this was to prevent evil spirits from entering. The post was usually fixed under a cross beam of the timber structure. Although the wood used for the beam was oak, the actual witch post was made of rowan or mountain ash. The usual position for these posts was just inside the doorway or forming the end post of the wooden partition. A St. Andrew's cross was incised at the top and beneath it were carved horizontal bands, varying from one to twelve. The use of a cross in the carving implies a belief in the magical properties of a cross to avert evil, and to afford protection against witches or any other hostile powers. It was believed that a witch could not enter beyond the post; nor while it stood could she lay a spell upon the hearth of the house. These witch posts spoke of the frequency of witch laying up to 1704 and when anyone in the parish was sorely distressed by their cattle dying from mysterious causes, they would discuss the matter with the parish priest and ask if anything could be done in regard to laying the power of the witch. The priest seems to have had the same credulity as the people, with the added credulity that he was possessed with power to assist them by laying the power of the witch. After this mysterious ceremony was over and the power of the witch was supposed to have been rendered nil, it was the custom of the priest to cut the Roman figure X on the upright oak post. This mark cut in the post by the priest meant that the witch's spell could not operate beyond this post.

Examples of some of these posts can be seen in the Ryedale Folk Museum at Hutton-le-Hole. Most are tenoned and peg-holed at the top, indicating where they were attached to a cross beam. At the bottom they were often drilled to take the supports of an inglenook seat. There are very few to be found other than in this area of north east Yorkshire. They are a part of the structure of the house, they are made of oak, and the carving is in the seventeenth century style. The one from Postgate Farm at Glaisdale is dated 1664. Supporting the theory of protection from witches, one of the rare cases in the Church Courts occurred in 1678 when Dorothy Cooke of Whitby was accused of bewitching a child to death. It would seem that the carved posts continued an ancient tradition carried on from medieval times and medieval houses, which may have derived the symbol of the cross from even earlier dwellings. This diagram shows the position of the witch post. A short passage is formed by a permanent screen on one side and the outer wall on the other. At the end of the screen stands the witch post which has the functional role in that it helps to support the cross beam of the smoke hood which overhangs the open hearth, but in the North Yorkshire Moors region it became a talisman with mystical powers effective against witchcraft. Once the occupants were past this post, they were safe from her evil powers. Undoubtedly the fixed wooden seat or settle which was typical behind the screen must have been the warmest and most comfortable spot to sit.

Why the number of horizontal bands on the witch post should vary was suggested to indicate the number of persons requiring protection. It seems that the witches complained about the installation of these posts in verse form:

'Oh Master. Oh Master, we can't do no good
She's got a witch cross made o' mountain ash wood.'

These posts besides preventing the entry of witches were also used for a repository—a crooked sixpence being kept in a hole at the centre of the post. When the butter would not turn, it was customary to take a knitting needle which was kept for the purpose in a groove at the top, and with it get out the sixpence and put it in the churn. This was supposed to neutralise the witchcraft.

THE SEVENTH TRUSTEE

A Story of Dales Witchcraft

by Arthur H. Whitaker

You've eeard o' Bert Frank and 'is cruck house at 'Utton;
For searchin' out crucks 'e war a fair glutton.
Well, 'e eeard frev a fellow called Tony, 'is friend
That a cruck 'ouse were fallin' ti bits called Stangend.

'E went ovver ti Raymond and said 'Shut up thi books
Wer gine off ti Danby ti pick up some crucks.'
They gat a few youths and set off wi' 'igh 'opes
An' their cars were fair brustin' wi' crowbars an' ropes.

They 'itched up their ropes ti t'crucks and tie beeams
An' Bert said 'This is the 'ouse of mi dreeams.'
They rave out the panellin', t'smoak-'ood an' all
An' Bert shouted 'Seea, there's a salt-box in t'wall.'

They'd gotten ti t'witch post just as the sun sank;
'Ah'm tekkin this 'oam in mi car' said Bert Frank.
So off gans aud Bert in 'is car wiv 'is post
But down cam a mist and t'aud beggar gat lost.

'E gat oot o' t'car an' fell slap in a ditch.
Then up cam a woman weer said 'Ah'm a witch.'
'Hey up' said aud Bert wi' all mad on his suit,
'Thoo can do me no 'arm; ah've a witch post in t'boot.'

At that t'aud witch let off sike a scrike;
An' just then Frank Weatherill passed by on 'is bike.
'By gow, Frank,' said Bertram, 'ah've gotten off t'track.'
'Deean't stop me,' said Frank, 'ah've got t'chimley on t'back.'

Seea Bert got back in tiv 'is car and set off,
When all iv a sudden 'e 'eeard a loud cough;
And there sittin' upright behind 'im on t'seeat
Were t'witch; an' she said 'Ah sall 'aunt tha to-neet.'

'Noo, listen,' said Bert, 'ah've tellt ye afooar
Wi t'witch post i' plaace thoo can't pass mi dooar;
But ah will tell tha what — if thi witchcraft tha'll lend
Ti get rid o' this mist — tha can go 'aunt Stangend.

'But 'aud on a minute, ah've just 'ad a thooart:
Ah can give tha a job—well, a job iv a sooart.
Ah'm biggin' a cruck 'ouse at 'Utton-le-'Ole;
Ah could build tha a hovel ti live in an' all.'

Well, t'witch opened t'window—it's truth as ah tell—
An' she waved 'er aud broomstick an' uttered a spell;
An' by gow within seconds that mist it were gone,
An' Bert an' t'aud woman tiv 'Utton sped on.

Noo, Eveline were capped when Bert opened the dooar
An' t'witch floated in wiv 'er broomstick on t'flooar.
'Weer's this?' she fair screeched, but Bert put 'er at ease,
'It's nobbut another o' t'Museum trustees.'

So now if you visit the Ryedale Folk Park
Don't stay in the Cruck House long after it's dark;
For round at the back there's a little thatched room,
And there sits the witch with her cat and her broom.

THE TALE OF THE OLD WITCH AND JOHNNY SIMPSON

THE following legend took place in Great Ayton on a dark and thundery night many years ago. Johnny Simpson was a young man with a great deal on his mind, and seemed totally oblivious to the gathering storm. His face was set and determined as he hurried over the Green to the tumbled-down cottage where Old Nanny lived—the witch of Ayton. He was practically there when he started to have second thoughts, wondering if maybe he should return home and let the events that had led him here tonight, take their natural course. Then he noticed the old lady through a crack in the door. She was moaning away to herself over the hob. Three times she spat as she dropped things into the pot from her lap, one by one, as she sang the following curse:

Fire cum, fire gan,
Curlin' smeeak keep out o' t'pan.
Ther's a teead i' t'fire, a frog on t'hob,
Here's t'heeart frev a crimson ask,
Here's a teeath fra t'heead
O' yan 'at's deead
'At nivver gat thruff his task;

Here's, prick'd i' blood, a maiden's prayer,
'At e'e o'man maunt see,
It's prick'd upon a jet warm mask
An' lapt aboot a breeght green ask
An' it's all fer him an' thee;
It boils, thoo'll drink,
He'll speeak, thoo'll think,
It boils, thoo'll see,
He'll speeak, thoo'll dee.

It was a spell that she was working and Johnny was getting very nervous as he was watching her. He was just about to leave when she suddenly stopped what she was doing, put the lid back on the pot and called out to him that she was not ready and would he let himself in —she had obviously been expecting him. 'Don't be frightened,' she said, 'I've been waiting for you. I know what you want and who you are. I've watched what she's done and I know what he does. You've come in a temper. I know. I know,' shrieked out old Nan.

She welcomed him in and invited him to tell his story—about how the girl he'd planned to marry had taken off with another man. John wanted to punish them and the old lady said that she could help him. Did he want them to die? To be blinded? John answered that he wanted them to go ahead and get married and from that moment on to have nothing but bad luck. He promised her anything if she could do this for him. She told him that all these things could be done, but instead she would tell him how to go about doing it himself. She then explained to John that he had to go to Holly garth and cross his hands from Ayton Bridge; then to turn his face without moving his feet, swing her broom three times around his head and wait for the owl to hoot three times thrice. He was then to start walking backwards being careful not to fall over because if he did he'd stay there all night. He had then to go to the churchyard and gather earth from the grave of someone that had committed suicide, and make it into a ball; gather moss scraped from a headstone; pluck a single blade of grass and while chewing it—wish all the nasty and evil things that he could think of onto the couple. John was then to hurry back to the Holly garth to the exact same place where he had stood before, work the moss and the ball of earth into the ground again wishing all the ill he could on the couple. When he'd done this he had to go to the old well and be sure to wash his hands, and to return her broom. With that she shut the door in his face.

John thought for a while and then decided to go ahead with the plan that very night. He did everything as he had been instructed, but he broke his promise to old Nan and did not wash his hands in the well or return her broom—instead he flung her broom into the river, leaving Ayton with a smile on his face. Breaking his word did not bother him at all. Then suddenly all around him he heard the strange flapping noise of wings, and saw strange faces and arms trying to grab him. He started to run, and he ran and ran straight into three night hags who told him that he was to be punished for breaking his word. They caught hold of John and flew off with him to the top of Roseberry. They warned him that he would pay for the curses he had made on Mary. The night hags then gave him a ten minute lead before they would start to hunt him down—the curse would be his if he lost the race, and if he went home to hide he would be dead before daylight. They gave him a stick and set him off. He ran as hard as he could but all the time he could hear them coming, shrieking in the air. He headed for Easby bank thinking that if he could reach Kildale Force he could wash the scent of the moss and soil from his hands. He just wanted to cross some running water thinking that that would set him free. Then John remembered the old witch's words—that while he had a foothold on the bridge nothing could harm him that night. He ran for his life towards the bridge, but in the dark he missed his way, stumbled and fell into the beck. The hags caught up with him, dragged him out and beat him leaving him almost dead. They left at the first sight of dawn, and John dragged himself to the bridge where old Nan was waiting for him. She reprimanded him for breaking his word but said she held no grudge and he could be rid of the curse he had inherited if he washed himself in the well every morning and night which he did for over five weeks until he had broken the spell. That night he slept peacefully—untroubled.

CORN DOLLIES

IT is thought that the first plaited corn dolly could have been cornucopia, for symbolically it has been used in pagan worship to represent continuing plenty. The story behind this symbol concerns Zeus, who was saved from death at the hands of his father Cronus, by being hidden in the cave of the nymphs. In return for this care he gave a goat's horn full to overflowing with the fruits of the earth, with the promise of an abundance to whosoever owned it. Old documents suggest that we in Britain at one time offered goats' horns on altars set up to honour the sun god Apollo. Maybe this is the time, of Roman occupation when the first plaited corn dollies were introduced to our isles.

Early farmers believed that the spirit of the goddess of fertility lived in the fields, in the ears of the growing plants. Her spirit would die if all the corn was cut and threshed, so the best, or last sheaf of the harvest was fashioned into a corn dolly (known as a 'dozzle' locally), to ensure her spirit's safe keeping until sowing time the next year. This protectress of the living, and awakener of new life was known by various names—the most widely known being Ceres, the corn spirit and Earth mother, which is why the corn idol was fashioned in the form of a doll (it was once called a 'kern-baby'). The making of this idol was an essential part of the fertility rites performed at the end of the harvest. There lingered here the idea of thankfulness for a harvest safely gathered in, and a hope for a successful new sowing perhaps too, a belief that the corn spirit would guard the stack from harm.

The corn dolly (harvest queen) was held on high on a pole which was decorated with grain and flowers and brought in from the fields accompanied by the singing and shouting of the harvesters. This pole was then reared up in the stack yard for the birds to eat during the winter. Locally it became known as the mell sheaf and it was always given pride of place at the harvest celebrations.

HORSE BRASSES

ONE of pre-historic man's dreads must have been the fear of the dark, firstly because of wild beasts and secondly because of evil spirits. From early times the moon was looked upon as a friendly being, and an amulet or charm in the shape of a full moon or crescent moon was deemed effective against evil. The earliest designs of these brasses were of the simple crescent shape cut from solid sheet brass—an emblem of the friendly moon. They were used initially as a charm, to avoid 'overlooking' by people with the evil-eye. The shining brass acts as a kind of lightning conductor taking the evil-eye away from the wearer. Eventually the plain crescent became an ornamental one. The oldest designs always incorporated the sign of the crescent moon. The luck traditionally associated with an old horseshoe was because it was iron (always valued) and also because it was in the form of a crescent.

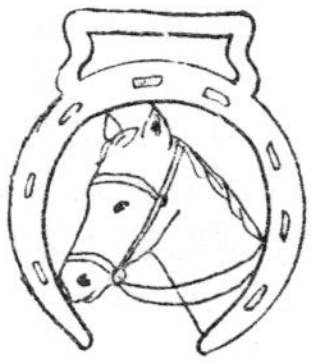

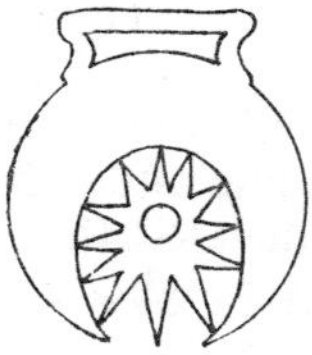

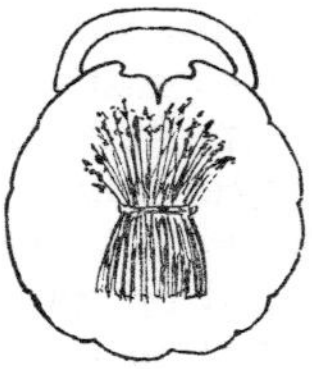

THE SERPENT OF HANDALE

SCAW WOOD at Handale is said to be named after a dragon-slaying youth of medieval times. The story is very similar to the better known one of St. George and the Dragon. In this case the dragon lived in the wood near a small Benedictine priory. This dragon was known as the Serpent of Handale and it had a particular weakness for the young ladies. And it was decided that something drastic had to be done and quickly. One young knight, called Scaw, was determined to slay the beast and save the rest of the female population, so dressed in his complete uniform of armour, Scaw set forth in search of the beast. When he found the dragon's cave deep in the woods, he struck a rock near the entrance and the beast came rushing out angered at being woken from sleep. It attacked the knight viciously with its poisonous sting and breathed fire from its nostrils onto the knight's armour. Just as Scaw's armour was becoming unbearably hot he managed to plunge his sword deep into the dragon's throat. The dragon perished—no more to prey on the young women of the district. And the young man received a bonus for his chivalrous deed (as well as having the wood named after him), because when he searched the dragon's cave, he found a beautiful girl. She was so grateful for her rescue that she offered the young knight her hand in marriage. He accepted. Scaw appears also to have had a weakness for the young ladies, and it would not have been at all chivalrous to refuse the request of a lady (besides, she was an earl's daughter and because of the marriage, he became a very wealthy and famous landowner).

HOBS

THERE are many legends in this area of 'Old Nick,' especially on the moors where there are remains of ancient stone circles, and strange 'mounds.' Old Nick often goes by the name of 'Hob,' and his image is replaced by that of a pixie or a hob-goblin. Almost every village seems to have had its Hob whose habits were in general kindly and helpful. The most well-known legend about Hob comes from the small fishing village of Runswick Bay, where a small cavern in the cliff wall is known as Hob-Hole. This was said to have been the home of one of these shaggy haired fairy creatures. Local people believed that the Hob could cure whooping cough so children suffering from the ailment were taken to this cave and the help of the Hob was sought by the parents reciting the rhyme:

Hob-hole Hob!
My bairn's gotten t'kink cough,
Tak 't off! Tak 't off!

And after that the child would improve. There seems to have been a number of remedies for curing whooping cough or 'kin-cough' as it was commonly called. If the people of this part of Yorkshire could not visit the Hob at Runswick Bay, then they would use an alternative cure, for example, they would pass the ailing child several times under a donkey, or they would go to live near a gasworks, but the visit to the Hob of Runswick seems a much more romantic notion.

HOB OF HART HALL

HART HALL at Glaisdale once had its own hob who lived there, threshed the corn by night, and then eventually left. This hob was kind and gentle and if there was any work to be done on the farm, he would come to the rescue, and in the morning the farmer would find that his corn had been threshed, dressed and stacked. The hob was never seen or heard doing his tasks but everyone knew that it was the work of the hob. Those working at the farm were very keen to catch a glimpse of him and spy on his activities.

One moonlight night, they heard him working and one of the lads crept to the door and looked through a hole in the boards, and there he saw a little brown man covered all over in hair without a stitch of clothing on his body. He was working hard at threshing the corn with a flail. The young lad watched for quite some time, amazed at the speed at which the little man was working. Eventually he crept away and told the others the things he had seen, describing the amazing energy of the 'little hairy man.' The cold winter nights were coming in and the folk at Hart Hall thought that they would make the hob something to wear to help keep him warm. So they made him a coarse shirt with a girdle and laid it out in the barn for the little man when he next came to work. As the days got colder it was said that the little hob was so cold that he was seen by the maid asleep on the fireside hob, where on being roused, he immediately fled to the butter churn. But seeing him during the day was very unusual, and it was quite a while before he made his next appearance in the barn. He saw the little garment and looked it over very carefully with a look

of disgust growing on his face. He expressed his dissatisfaction in the following rhyme:

Gin Hob mun hae nowght but a hardin' hamp,
He'll coom nae mair, nowther to berry nor stamp.

The little man obviously thought that for all his hard work he was entitled to more than a rough, coarse garment to keep him warm and so the hob left Hart Hall forever, and the folk living there had to thresh their own corn.

JEANIE OF MULGRAVE WOODS

ANOTHER story from this area concerning an ethereal creature a certain fairy named Jeanie, who lived deep in the Mulgrave Woods, near Whitby. Jeanie was a very happy and peaceful fairy, gentle in form and manner, but she had a terrible temper when aroused. Her peaceful bliss spent pursuing an untroubled life of fairy-like tasks was soon broken by a curious young man. He was the son of a local farmer and he had heard rumours about the existence of Jeanie in the woods, and he was determined to discover if there was any truth in this rumour. He searched the woods methodically and eventually found her hiding place. Her peace shattered and her seclusion invaded by the clumsy quest of this young man so aroused the temper of Jeanie that she rushed out at the young man, shouting curses and flourishing her wand. The young farmer was quite taken aback by this behaviour, and soon discovered that his courage was not as strong as his curiosity, so he turned on his heels and fled on his horse. But Jeanie did not give up that easily and pursued him relentlessly, getting nearer and nearer. The young man was terrified and convinced that some awful fate would befall him if the fairy ever caught up with him. Then he remembered the old folk tale that fairies were not supposed to be able to cross over water, so he headed his horse towards the nearest stream and started to cross it just as Jeanie caught up with him. The young man had remembered his folk tales well because Jeanie could not follow him, but she did manage to strike the animal's rear end with her wand and the noble beast perished in the water, but the young farmer survived. He managed to return home, horseless and rather wet—his curiosity having been somewhat dampened.

STAITHES MERMAIDS

THERE is a delightful legend that appears to be peculiar to the small picturesque fishing village of Staithes. It concerns the sea and two of its mythical inhabitants. The incident happened many many years ago when Staithes was just a simple fishing community and not a popular tourist attraction like it is now. Two mermaids had been caught in the middle of a fierce storm many miles from their home. They were tired and exhausted from the continual buffeting of the waves and were greatly relieved when they spied the small village nestling at the bottom of the cliffs. They used their last few ounces of strength to drag themselves onto the shore where they collapsed. When the two mermaids regained consciousness, they found themselves surrounded by staring curious eyes. The people were very suspicious of these strange beings and fearing that they might do them harm, they had the two mermaids imprisoned. They were held captive for many months and the people grew used to them and did not fear them as much as they had done in the beginning, and so gradually the guard on the two mermaids was relaxed. They took advantage of this and managed to gain their liberty. They made straight for the sea and when they eventually reached its safety, one of the mermaids turned round and stared at the village that had been her prison for these last few long months. She was so angry and annoyed at the way that they had been treated that she put a curse on the village, saying, 'The sea shall flow to Jackdaw's Well.' The Jackdaw's Well mentioned in the curse is no longer to be found in Staithes—it has long since disappeared, but it was once sited to the landward side of Seaton Garth. Jackdaw's Well derived its name from the large number of birds of that species that frequented the area. It could be said that the curse of the mermaid came true because since the incident all those years ago the sea has already encroached upon thirteen houses that used to stand between the shore and the well.

BOGGLES

AN old north Yorkshire term for a ghost or a phantom was a boggle. Just outside Robin Hood's Bay there is a ravine running down to the sea which is known by the name of Boggle Hole—no doubt having some phantom inhabitant. There is also just outside Grosmont a place once known as Boggle House, which was said to be haunted by a ghost of an apprentice tailor. He haunted this house until he became homeless when the house was destroyed. The story of how this house became haunted in the first instance runs as follows. Boggle House was owned by a tailor and the young man of the story was his apprentice. They would travel around the neighbouring farms together making up orders on the spot. They were kept very busy and most of the day and the evening was spent in the sewing and the making up of various garments. They had little free time but what they had was taken up with drinking and playing cards. In fact the tailor had an obsession with card playing and he made sure that he very rarely, if ever, lost a game. One night the tailor and his wife invited friends round to the house to play cards and they could not quite make up a complete school

The giant of Horcum.

and so the apprentice was invited in to make up the numbers. But the apprentice had heard that his master was a hard player and so he watched him very carefully and noticed that he was cheating. He immediately rose to his feet and accused the couple in front of their friends. The game was discontinued and everyone went home—that is except the apprentice. The tailor and his wife were furious with him and no one quite knows for certain what happened next, but the young apprentice was never seen again, leastways not by anyone other than the couple. The ghost of the apprentice made sure that they would never have a minute's peace again, or that they would ever cheat anyone else again.

THE HOLE OF HORCUM

THERE are many tales involving the formation of the Hole of Horcum and one involves the Mulgrave area again. In the Mulgrave woods crumbling towers and arches and broken-down walls are all that is left of a once magnificent fortress called Old Mulgrave Castle. The legend says the builder of this fortress was a twelve foot giant named Wade. He was one of the conspirators responsible for the death of King Ethelred and he built Mulgrave Castle to protect himself from the revenging allies of the murdered king. Wade, together with his wife, built both Mulgrave Castle and Pickering Castle. They shared the work using local stones on their lands—the only difficulty being that between them they possessed only one hammer. And when one or other of them wanted to borrow the hammer or more stones, they would call out to each other and throw the various materials to each other over the 23 miles. The hammer on one occasion was thrown with such force and inaccuracy that it fell short of its target causing a large hole in the ground, hence the formation of the Hole of Horcum. And somewhere along the main Whitby to Pickering road there can still be seen some large stones which also fell short in their journey from Mulgrave Castle to Pickering Castle.

The Roman Road, Wade's Causeway, is also said to be the work of the giant and his wife. Wade laid the stones for his wife to cross the moors to milk her cows. She provided the labouring work by carrying the stones in her apron. Despite his great size Wade eventually met his death in a battle, and his body was brought back to Mulgrave where he was buried. There are two gravestones twelve feet apart to mark the head and foot of the giant's grave on top of a hill just north of the castle, called Wade's Stone.

Another story about the giant hollow of Horcum concerns the Devil who was supposedly to have scooped up a great handful of earth to throw at his wife during an argument. It is said that one can still see the marks of his fingers on the side of the hole. This earth moving antic is also attributed to the giant Wade who was also involved in an argument—this time with a neighbouring giant. During the course of the quarrel Wade dug up a great spadeful of earth and threw it at his adversary. The large pile of earth and rocks landed miles away to form the cone-shaped hill called Blakey Topping.

This great hollow also goes by the name of 'The Devil's Punchbowl.' Certainly the Devil has always had some association with this hole. But the alternative name could have been derived from the days when the stagecoach passed that way, pausing for refreshment and a change of horses at the nearby inn where bowls of punch were brewed. This inn still exists high on the North Yorkshire Moors under the name of the *Saltersgate Inn*. It is still as isolated and bleak as it was in those early coaching days. A peat fire which had been kept alight for nearly 200 years once burnt in the kitchen. Tradition says that the Devil on one of his visits to this area was passing by the inn on a particularly rough night and called in for warmth. But he was met only by hostility and directly exorcised by a local priest who presumably was also just passing at the time. Satan, rather than face the terrible weather outside is said to have fled into the kitchen. A peat fire was immediately lit in order to keep him there, and it was in this endlessly smouldering hearth that he remained imprisoned ever since.

ROSEBERRY TOPPING

THIS conical hill near Guisborough, because of its detached position and superior elevation, commands in all directions a prospect at once extensive and interesting, and serves as a landmark to navigators. At the top of this hill from a large rock there issues a fountain of very clear water to which the following tradition is attached.

The story goes back to the time when King Oswald was king of Northumbria. He very much wanted a son and was overjoyed when his wife gave birth to a male child. The baby was named after the king and to celebrate the birth of the young Oswald, the king sent for all the wise men and magicians in the country to come to his court to visit his son and to predict his future. After seeing the child all the wise men arrived at the same conclusion—that the new born prince would not live to see his first birthday. They all agreed that when he was half a year old he would be drowned. On receiving this news the king and queen were extremely upset and determined to do all in their power to see that the unfortunate occurrence did not take place. They decided to take their son to the top of a hill for his

Oswald, ill-fated son of the king of Northumbria.

security, and so he was brought to Roseberry. A small cell was constructed out of the rock near the top of this hill, in order to prevent the prophesied unhappy death. But the young prince was indeed fated to die at six months of age, for a flowing stream dissolved the rocks of the young prince's cell and he was drowned. The distraught queen had her baby buried in Tivotdale (Osmotherley) church, but her grief and sorrow were such that she soon followed him, and was, according to her wishes, laid by her beloved child. The heads of the mother and son, cut in stone, may be seen at the east end of the church; and from a saying of the people, 'Os by his mother lay'—hence the village of Tivotdale changed its name to Osmotherley.

The following poem commemorates this story:

Ah! why do the walls of the castle today
No longer resound with the strains of delight?
And why does the harp of the minstrel so gay
Now rest in the gloom and the stillness of night?

But late as I travers'd these vallies long,
How high 'mid the air stream'd the banners of joy!
While the birth of prince Oswin, the boast of the song
Gave mirth to each heart, as it beam'd in each eye.

What stranger art thou, who, in Cleveland so fair,
Of the fate of prince Oswin canst yet be untold?
How an old hoary sage had foreshown the young heir
By water should die when but half a year old!

His mother, all eager her offspring to save,
To Ottenberg high, with the morn did repair.
Still hoping to rescue her son from the grave,
For well did she know that no water was there.

But how powerless and vain in a mortal's design,
Opposed to that will which can never recede:
Who shall pull down the bright orb of heaven divine,
And raise up a meteor his rays to exceed?

Fatigued, by ceaseless exertion opprest,
At length they arrive near the brow of the hill,
In whose shades on the moss they resign them to rest,
Now fearless of fate as unconscious of ill.

Not long in soft slumbers the fond mother lay,
Ere arous'd by a dream which dire horrors betide,
But, O God, who can paint her wild grief and dismay,
When she saw her lov'd baby lie drown'd by her side!

On the proud steep of Ottenberg still may be found,
That spring which arose his sad doom to complete;
And oft on its verge sit the villagers round,
In wonder recording the fiat of fate.

For this the walls of the castle today,
No longer resound with the strains of delight;
And for this does the harp of the bard once so gay,
Now rest in the gloom of the stillness of night.

KITTY OF FARNDALE

FARNDALE is a small picturesque village nestling in the north Yorkshire moors, famous for its daffodils. So this macabre little story originating here seems somewhat out of place. It involves a young girl called Kitty who was very much in love with a wealthy farmer's son. He pledged his love for her and talked of marriage until he discovered that she was pregnant. He denied responsibility, refused to marry her and ended the relationship. Kitty was distraught. She loved him. She had no one to turn to and pleaded with him to meet her once more at their secret rendezvous, hoping that she might be able to make him change his mind. After many tears the young man eventually agreed to meet Kitty to talk things over again when he had had time to think. As fate would have it, on the appointed night there was a terrible storm in the valley, and Kitty waited in vain for her lover to meet her. A local farmer saw her waiting in the rain and guessed the reason. He told her that he had seen a horseman riding off towards town—in the opposite direction. From his description of the young rider Kitty knew that it was her lover. She was convinced that she had been betrayed and deserted, and left alone to bear her child and her shame. And so the distraught girl tore off all her clothes and threw herself into the fierce raging torrents of the flooded river. It was a few days later that the body was found, by the ford, after the swollen river had abated a little. Ironically Kitty was not the only one to have been claimed a victim of the storm—for only a few yards from the place where they found her body, they discovered the body of her drowned lover. He had in his pocket a new wedding ring which he had just bought at the nearby town, and he was returning to meet her when he had been caught by the storm filled river.

His body was buried in the local churchyard, but because Kitty had committed suicide she was not allowed to be buried near him, but had to be buried at the crossroads. Kitty's was a restless spirit and her ghost haunted the ford. And each year she would appear by the ford as the river claimed yet another victim on the anniversary of her death. This greatly troubled the local village people, especially one man who was disturbed from his sleep by a vivid dream. He woke his wife and together they crept out into the night and dug up the remains of Kitty's grave and re-buried her in the graveyard, to be at peace with her lover. From that moment onwards the ghost of Kitty was never seen again and the annual death toll ended.

Kitty of Farndale.

HART LEAP

ON Glaisdale Rigg, near a spot where no fewer than eight paths meet, stand two stones known as Hart Leap. The distance between them is fourteen yards. Tradition said that a hart, hard pressed in the chase by pursuing deer hounds, made that extraordinary leap in a last desperate effort to escape. The hart is said to have left behind its footprints on the soft ground. These stone posts were fixed in the place where this long distance jump took place many centuries ago. The story is as follows:

There was once a big black hart known locally as 'The Mickle Black Hart of Threllkeld,' because of its size and colour. This hart had been chased often but no one was ever able to get anywhere near him. One hunter was determined to catch him at any price, even if it meant that he would never hunt again or had to pledge his very soul. He organised fresh horses and fresh hounds to meet him along the route. The great day came and the hart was sighted. The chase was on. Horses became tired. Hounds became tired, but the hart seemed to be as fresh as ever. Twice the hunter changed both his horse and his hounds, but they were no nearer to the hart, and night was starting to fall. The hunter was getting very annoyed when suddenly a figure appeared beside him seated on a great black horse. The hunter wished that he had such a magnificent beast under him to help him catch the hart. The stranger sensed this and asked him what he would give for his horse. The hunter replied that he would give him all that he possessed in the world. The stranger said he wanted more than that and the frustrated hunter replied, 'All I have in the world and all that there is in the next.' This was agreed on condition that the hunter never hung the hart's head in his own hall. They exchanged mounts and the hunter was away, renewed with a fresh vigour and determination. He closed the gap between himself and the hart and soon it was panting and slowing down before making one desperate last bound, when it fell headlong and died. The story does not end here because the hunter soon regretted the day that he had made the bargain, because he could not even show off his trophy, or his pride by hanging the head of the hart in his own hall.

The hounds that accompanied the hunter on this last final venture died in mysterious circumstances and are said to still haunt the moors searching for the headless hart. They are known as the Gaabrel Ratchet (Gaabrel means corpse and Ratchet means a hound which hunts by scent—hence Gaabrel Ratchet—the Corpse Hounds). It was reckoned very unlucky to hear the Gaabrel Ratchet for if you did, it was supposed to presage your own death or that of someone close to you within the year. The way to prevent this happening if you were unlucky enough to come into contact with the hounds, was to throw yourself promptly onto your face and wrap your coat around your head so that you do not hear the beating of the hoofs or the yelping of the hounds.

WOLF PIT SLACK

THE name of Wolf Pit Slack is the name given to a hollow in the moor, which can be found between the dales of Danby and Little Fryup on a narrow neck of the moorland ridge. Tradition has it that it was at this particular narrow neck of moorland that the wild animals that once commonly infested the dales chose to make their crossing place from Danby Dale to Little Fryup Dale. Among the wild animals that frequented the dales once were wolves. And these wolves had the habit similar to that of the smaller wild animals that survive in the area today—such as foxes who have their own favourite haunts and crossing places, and this particular area was the favourite haunt and crossing place of the wolf.

There is record of bounty being paid on the heads of wolves captured, for example in the fourteenth century in Baisdale (not more than five or six miles from Wolf Pit Slack) land rents were paid by means of so many heads of wolves, in order that the country might be freed from the dangers to both man and animal from these savage beasts. This being the case it is more than somewhat likely that Wolf Pit Slack inherited its name from its use as a favourite trapping ground for wolves.

FATHER POSTGATE

FATHER Postgate has been a legend of these moorland areas for 300 years—a martyr for his religion. Nicholas Postgate was born in Egton Bridge in 1599 and it was to this area that he returned as a travelling priest. As the landed gentry slowly died out, the number of priests working from country houses lessened and the number of travelling priests increased. This is what happened to Father Postgate. This district had a great tradition of priest harbouring in these troubled times. This was not too difficult due to the isolation of the area which was then much more heavily wooded than it is now. (Egton means 'the place of the oaks.') Whitby was the nearest town and this was itself so isolated that, long after Father Postgate's time, it was known that many criminals came here to avoid the law.

Some time about 1665 Father Postgate started to offer mass in the building which became famous as the Egton Mass House halfway down Egton Bank. The chapel was a small separate section of the loft. There were no windows into the room, just a small hole in the thatching so that a watch could be kept for pursuivants. The small room was only fifteen feet long by ten feet wide; the height being only five and a half feet. It was very difficult to hold a service for more than a few people, but this was all they had.

Charles II had pledged the Quakers that if they lived peacefully none of them would suffer for their religion's sake. Yet for men such as Hyde, non-conformity in religion was only one of the faces of sedition. Against Quakers and Dissenters generally, laws were passed which made it impossible for them to live peacefully. Those who did not obey the law were said to oppose it and many were driven to rebel. The Quakers Act of 1662 forbade the assembly of more than a few persons for private worship not in keeping with the Act of Uniformity. Dissenters became law breakers simply by meeting to pray together and perform the simplest acts of worship. Slowly the hatred of Dissenters passed onto Roman Catholics. It was at this time that Father Postgate was betrayed and arrested. He was committed

to gaol in York. On the 6th of March 1679 he stood trial charged with being a priest. His death was fixed for the 7th of August. At his death he stated that he died for his religion, not for any plot; that he forgave all who had a part in bringing him to death; that he prayed for the King, and sought the forgiveness of all whom he might have offended. He suffered the usual hanging, drawing and quartering which was inflicted on priests. The top joint of the forefinger and thumb of each hand was cut off, since he had often held the Sacred Host in them during the 'superstition' of mass. The skeleton hands have been preserved—the right hand being at St. Cuthbert's, Old Elvet, Durham, and the left at Ampleforth. Father Postgate died because he was a priest, ironically betrayed by one of his own county-men; one whom he had lived 'among,' to whose circumstances he conformed as to dress, diet and lodging.

Thomas Ward of Danby wrote of Father Postgate in this extract from his *England's Reformation:*

Nor spar'd they Father Postket's blood,
A reverend priest, devout and good,
Whose spotless life in length was spun
To eighty years and three times one.
Sweet his behaviour, grave his speech,
He did by good example teach;

THE PLOUGH STOTS

IN the iron mining villages in the Cleveland district of north Yorkshire traditional dances, performed with thirty to forty inch long swords made of steel or wood, are still practised by teams of six or eight men. These sword dances are of the long-sword variety and are thought to be of Scandinavian origin, probably brought to these parts when the Danes invaded the area. There are many local variations but they all seem to involve the mock decapitation of a leader. The dances are round dances and are ritualistic in origin. Many villages in the area had teams of sword dancers, for example: Staithes, Flamborough, Sleights and Egton, but the most famous for its company of Sword Dancers and Plough Stots is the village of Goathland.

'Stot' is the name for a bullock and this name became transferred to the young man who pulled the plough in the procession on Plough Monday (the first Monday after Twelfth Night—when the ploughman's feast occurs). This old time procession of rustics would come into town—the men acting as oxen and dragging the plough. They wore shirts over their jackets, and were decked out with sashes and rosettes of bright colours. These jolly 'fellows who follow the plough' first went to mass and then began their rounds of the villages and towns to collect money to continue their secular festivities. The picturesque sword dance and traditional music of the 'Stot's Fool Plough' was one of the outstanding events of Yuletide.

The following is an extract from the *Cleveland Fool Plough* play. (Performers: about a dozen, dressed grotesquely, with lath-swords and streamers. The captain, dressed in cocked hat, forms a circle by swinging his sword around.)

Clown: Good gentlemen all, to our Captain take heed,
And hear what he's got for to sing;
He's lived among music these forty long years,
And drunk of the helicon spring.

Captain: Six actors I have brought
Who were ne'er on a stage before;
But they will do their best,
And they can do no more.

The first that I call in
He is a squire's son;
He's like to lose his sweetheart
Because he is too young.
But though he is too young,
He has money for to rove,
And he will spend it all
Before he'll lose his love.
(Marches around. Fiddle, and chorus fal lal de ral.)

The next I call in
He is a tailor fine;
What think you of this work?
He made this coat of mine! (Coat full of holes.)
So comes good master Snip,
His best respects to pay;
He joins us in our trip
To drive dull care away. (Walks round.)

The next I do call in,
The prodigal son is he;
By spending of his gold
He's come to poverty.
But though he all has spent,
Again he'll wield the plow,
And sing right merrily
As any of us now. (Relic of mystery play.)

Next comes a skipper bold,
He'll do his part right weel;
A clever blade I'm told
As ever pozed a keel.
He is a bonny lad,
As you must understand;
It's he can dance on deck,
As you'll see him dance on land. (Dances.)

To join us in this play
Here comes a jolly dog,
Who's sober all the day—
If he can get no grog.
But though he likes his grog,
As all his friends do say,
He always likes it best
When other people pay. (Marches reeling.)

Last I come in myself,
The leader of this crew;
And if you'd know my name,
My name it is True Blue.

Clown: My mother was burnt for a witch,
My father was hanged on a tree,
And it's because I'm a fool
There's nobody meddled wi' me.

(Dance: cross swords; intertwine; confusion; quarrel; parson rushes in, and is killed.)

Captain: Alas! Our parson's dead,
And on the ground is laid;
Some of us will suffer for't
Young men, I'm sore afraid.

Squire's Son: I'm sure 'twas none of me,
I'm clear of that crime;
'Twas him that follows me
That drew his sword so fine.

Tailor: I'm sure it was not me,
I'm clear of the fact;
'Twas him that follows me
That did this dreadful act.

Prodigal: I'm sure 'twas none of me,
Who say't be villains all;
For both my eyes were closed,
When this good priest did fall.

Clown: Cheer up, cheer up, my bonny lads,
And be of courage brave,
We'll take him to his church,
And bury him in the grave.

Captain: Oh, for a doctor—
Ten pound for a doctor, oh!

Doctor: Here am I.

Captain: Doctor, what's your fee?

Doctor: Ten pounds is my fee, but £9 19s 11¾d
I will take from thee.

Clown: There's gen-er-os-i-ty!

Doctor: I'm a doctor, a doctor rare,
Who travels much at home;
My famous pills they cure all ills,
Past, present, and to come.
My famous pills, who'd be without,

They cure the plague, the sickness, and gout,
Anything but a love-sick maid,
If you're one, my dear, you're beyond my aid!

(Points to any girl; sprinkles meal from a box on the parson's face, and says:)

Take a little of my nif-naf,
Put it on your tif-taf;
Parson rise up and preach again,
The doctor says you are not slain.

(Parson sneezes, and rises up.)

Captain: Our play is at an end,
And now we'll taste your cheer;
We wish you a merry Christmas
And a happy New Year.

Clown: And your pockets full of brass,
And your cellars full of beer. (All dance.)

A team consists of six men generally and there is usually a 'captain' or a 'king.' The Plough Stots are gaily bedecked in uniforms of pink and blue. The 'pinks' and 'blues' were old political colours of the day. There are five round figures in the Goathland set of sword dances and a 'No Man's Jig' in addition. Here is a version of the opening song of the Goathland Plough Stots—used a hundred years ago:

The Goathland Plough Stots

Here's a host of us all
From Goathland go we
We are going a rambling
The country for to see
The country for to see.

Some pastime for to make
So freely you will give to us,
As freely we will take!
And now you see us all
Dressed in our grand array
Think of us what you will
Music, strike up and play!

The dances are fascinating affairs of clockwise and anti-clockwise hitch-stepping, swords going up and under and over in a complicated pattern of rolls, locks, single-unders and double-unders. The 'clash,' the increasing rhythm and the mock beheading all suggest that the dances have their origin in pagan times. The culminating feature of each dance-figure is the locking of the swords into an hexagonal shape (or an octagonal shape as in the 'No Man's Jig'), and the elevation of the lock or 'rose' by the king of the dancers. The individual dances represent the traditional story of death and resurrection—without tragedy. The central theme is unvarying—new hopes and new beginnings, as a farmer will plough his land at the beginning of a new year to produce new fruit and a plentiful harvest.

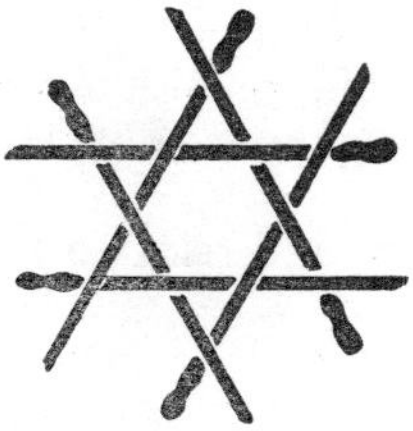

If on completion of their dances any observer refused to contribute to the collectors (Toms) then the plough boys would turn a furrow of earth on his lawn or garden in retaliation. In many villages the custom of sword dancing has died out, but not here—in Goathland it has been revived and commemorated in the following poem by F. W. Dowson:

T' Pleeaf Stots

Here they cum, tidaay seea grand,
Runnin', lowpin', sooards i' hand!
Rooases, ribbins, cooats sea sthrange,
Hoose ti hoose they're gahin ti raange.

Last back-end when neets was dark,
All t'lads set theirsens ti wark—
Leearnt their steps, an' showed their airt,
Watchin' t'awd fooaks deea their pairt.

Hoo they thried an' thried ageean,
Thowt this nivver wad be deean!
Then they drissed i' sike fine cleeas
Fancy suits frae heead ti teeas.

'Blues' an' 'Pinks' is allus pets.
Seean theease danced i' tweea fine sets.
Watch 'em plet at last their sooards,
Just when theease seeam flung all rooads.

Here's t'awd woman an' t'awd man!
Peak'd aboon 'em sits a cloon.
Sike queer 'stots' an' 'actin'' teea—
Sum on t'deearstean, sum i' t'fleear!

Off they gan awaay ower't green
Sike a show, was't ivver seen?
Noo they're i' t'foad garth ti start,
Ivvry yan seea glad at heart.

Roond an' roond they dance i' t'ring
Then they tawk, an' sumtahmes sing,
Grand awd fiddler! Whea can beat
Tunes like thine is despert greeat.

Laugh an' dance, an' shoot an' sing,
This is t'daay ti hae yer fling.
Keep t'awd plaay up ivvery year,
Nowt else like it, we're all seear.

Tunes played on the fiddle varied considerably, but the following are often used: Pop Goes the Weasle; Careless Sally; Grandfather's Clock; Corn Rigs; When Irish Eyes Are Smiling (for No Man's Jig).

THE GYTRASH OF GOATHLAND

MANY many years ago when Arthur was said to rule in Camelot, the vale of the Murk Esk was held by Julian of Goathland. He wanted to build himself a castle and chose the beautiful area that is still called Julian Park even to this very day. He was a hard and cruel man who did not believe in God; instead he worshipped Woden and Thor. He was an evil lord hated by all the countryside and the reasons for this can be seen as the story unfolds. It was an old pagan belief that any great house or temple in order to stand the test of time must be built with life in it, and so Julian swore by the Ravens of Woden that whosoever was the best beloved of the maidens of Eskdale should be walled up in the foundations of his keep and to be left there to perish miserably. The girl chosen was Gytha the beautiful daughter of Gudrun of the Mill. Julian sent his men to seize her. The people of Goathland were very angry and followed the soldiers to the castle where they begged Julian to spare the girl. He simply laughed at them and to show them that he was master, he dragged Gudrun out of the crowd and commanded that he himself should build the wall for his daughter's tomb. Gudrun refused saying he would rather die. He was taken away and tortured most cruelly until eventually he had neither the strength nor the will to refuse. When there remained two stones left to be placed—a beaker of water and a loaf of bread were placed by the girl's side, along with her spindle and spinning wheel. Julian did not want

The Gytrash and the spinning maiden.

the girl to be idle while she was dying. An so the wall was finished and the crying girl entombed.

The Hermit of Eskdaleside even visited Julian and asked him to repent. Julian merely laughed him to scorn and then set his dogs on him. The holy man barely escaped with his life. On the anniversary of the girl's entombment Julian was busy planning extensions to the castle when he heard a great wailing which came nearer and nearer. Julian found he could not move. The door opened and a white figure clothed in the garments which Gytha had worn came into the room carrying a spindle in her hand. The girl did not speak but simply came over and stood at Julian's bed. She stood for a short while and then stretched out her hand holding the spindle over his feet. Three times she moved the spindle over the base of the bed and as she moved it, it seemed to him that invisible threads were being wound about his feet and ankles, threads which he could not break. Slowly the wailing stopped and the figure slowly disappeared. When Julian tried to get up he found that he could hardly walk. There was no life in his dead feet and for a year he shuffled around until the same night came around again.

And Julian heard the wailing again. This time the girl held the spindle over his knees, moved it three times and again he seemed to be bound with the same invisible threads. For the whole of the next year he was dead from the knees down. Julian was in such a plight that he sent for the Hermit of Eskdaleside and asked him to pray for him and if he did, then he would turn Christian and build a church for the people. The Hermit did what he could but nothing seemed to work. Each year on the appointed night the girl appeared and with her deadly spindle wound the invisible threads a little higher than the last time. For ten years Julian died slowly from the feet upwards until eventually he died during the night of a great storm. It was on that very night that the Gytrash was first seen.

The Gytrash was said to be the evil spirit of Julian. It was an enormous black goat with eyes that burned like live coals and it also possessed horns tipped with fire. The appearance of this strange being became very frequent and caused fear and panic in the people of the area. People would hear it behind them and if the goat ever overtook them then the next day they would be struck by a strange malady and die. But the Gytrash was not the only terror—the spirit of the Spinning Maid was still unlaid. At midnight on every anniversary of her death, the same wailing sounds were heard to come from the keep of the castle and that year whosoever was the most beautiful in the area was sure to die. The people were so persecuted that they turned to the Hermit again for help but to no avail. The Church having failed them, the distressed people called to the Spaewife of Fylingdales who was considered to be the most competent witch in those parts. After a while she told them that deliverance was to be found in a proper interpretation of the words, 'Tane to tither.' For weeks this puzzle was debated. Eventually one of the men gathered that it must mean that they should somehow set one of the phantoms to deal with the other, and that perhaps the magic threads of the maid could bind the Gytrash.

It was well known that these Gytrashes had a particular liking for the newly buried corpses, from which it was supposed that they drew their life and so they were determined to lure the Gytrash by means of a mock funeral into the place that they had prepared for him—the Killing Pits. Once they had lured him there, they wondered how they could get the maid to spin her threads around him and so they consulted the witch again. She told them that they need have no fear if the proper precautions were taken, for she said that there existed a mortal enmity between the Maid and the Gytrash. All they had to do was lay a trail of honey from the castle to the pits and sprinkle it with corn and salt. A Mell Baby was made from the last of the harvest, dressed in corpse clothes and placed in a coffin. This coffin was carried to the Pits a little before midnight. At exactly twelve the Gytrash appeared and then disappeared into the pit, shortly followed by the maid. She began to weave her magic thread over the goat. From the pit came a terrible cry and the sides of the pit began caving in burying the beast alive. The maid smiled, dropped her spindle and gradually faded away into the moonlight. Neither of them were ever seen again.

ROBIN HOOD

IT was during the reign of Richard I (The Lionheart) that we first hear of Robin Hood, the most famous of England's traditional archers. It was said of him that he 'was indeed an arch robber, but the gentlest thief that ever was.' It appears that his real name was Robert Fitzooth and that he was a man of quality, probably in the succession for the earldom of Huntingdon. Although he lived generally in the Nottingham area he had connections with the Whitby district. Charlton wrote in 1779 in *The History of Whitby and of Whitby Abbey* that when the crimes of Robin Hood 'became so numerous, and the outcries against him so loud, as almost to alarm the whole nation, parties of soldiers were sent down from London to apprehend him; And then it was, that, fearing for his safety, he found it necessary to desert his usual haunts, and retreating northwards, to cross the moors that surrounded Whitby . . . the chief place of his resort at those times to which he communicated his name, and which is still called Robin Hood's Bay.'

The Whitby coast was an ideal place for Robin to take refuge because there was the wild North Sea on one side and the inhospitable moors on the other. He made many friends in the area and there was always a good supply of several fishing boats that he could use to escape to the sea if he was being pursued. It was probably thanks to this area that Robin Hood was never caught.

A Scarborough tradition tells how the hero being bored with forest life decides to go and visit Scarborough, in the poem *The Noble Fisherman; Or Robin Hood's Preferment'*:

'Therefore I will to Scarborough go,
That I a fisherman brave may be.'

He joined the crew of a fishing boat, but being ignorant of the ways of the sea, he neglected to bait his hooks before throwing them overboard.

'When others cast in their baited hooks,
The bare line into the sea cast he.'

'It will be long,' said the master then,
Ere this great lubber do thrive on the sea;
I'le assure you he shall have no part of our fish,
For in truth he is no part worthy.'

Robin Hood.

He made amends when a French man o' war attacked the boat.

'Master, tye me to the mast,' saith he,
'That at my mark I may stand fair,
And give me my bent bow in my hand,
And never a Frenchman will I spare.'

Robin led the crew in boarding the raider, killed her captain and captured a vast sum of gold which he presented to the poor fishermen.

'It will be so, as I have said,
And, with this gold, for the opprest,
And habitation I will build,
Where they shall live in peace and rest.'

This probably referred to the village of Robin Hood's Bay.

Other references to the tradition of Robin Hood in north east Yorkshire are mentioned by the Whitby historian Dr. Young who said that 'according to tradition Robin Hood and his trusty mate, Little John, went to dine with one of the abbots of Whitby, and being desired by the abbot to try how far each of them could shoot an arrow, they both shot from the top of the abbey, and their arrows fell on the west side of Whitby Laithes, beside the lane leading from thence to Stainsacre; that of Robin Hood falling on the north side of the lane, and that of Little John about a hundred feet further, on the south side of the lane. In the spot where Robin's arrow is said to have lighted stands a stone pillar about a foot square, and four feet high; and a similar pillar, two and a half feet high, marks the place where John's arrow fell. The fields on the one side are called "Robin Hood Closes" and those on the other "Little John Closes." They are so termed in the conveyance, dated in 1713 from Hugh Cholmley Esq.'

Other stories of this arrow shooting episode say that Robin Hood shot an arrow from Stoupe Brow Beacon right across the Bay to mark the site of the present town of Robin Hood's Bay, but like most stories they are usually based on some elements of fact, and it is highly probable that Robin Hood did have connections with the picturesque fishing village which bears his name. A local song about Robin Hood's Bay called *Stow (Stoupe) Brow to Bay* is said to also be based on fact. Many of the locals assert that the gravestone mentioned in the song still exists in the old churchyard, but no one can find it, although many of the old stones are indecipherable now. The song is as follows:

Stow Brow to Bay

In Stow Brow, in Stow Brow a damsel did dwell,
She loved a young sailor, he loved her as well.
He promised to marry her when back he did return,
But mark what hard fortune all on them did frown.

As they were a-sailing a storm did arise,
The moon was overshadowed and dismal was the sky,
The wind it blew a hurricane and the billows loud did roar,
Which tossed these poor sailors all on the lee shore.

As they were a-swimming, a-swimming for their lives,
Some of them were single men and some of them had wives,
This poor unfortunate young man, who happened to be one,
Instead of being married he found a watery grave.

Oh when this shocking news reached this young damsel's ears,
She fell a-wringing of her hands and a-tearing of her hair,
Crying, 'Oh you cruel billows come wash my love on shore,
That I might behold his sweet features once more.'

As she was coming to Robin Hood's Bay,
She spied a drown sailor, all on the sands he lay.
She stepped up to him and a-mazing she did stand,
For she knew it was her own true love by the marks on his hands.

She kissed him, she blessed him ten thousand times o'er;
She kissed him, she blessed him ten thousand times the more,
Crying, 'How happy and contented I could lay down by his side.'
And a few more moments after, this fair maid she died.

In Robin Hood's Bay churchyard this young couple lay,
A verse on their tombstone is there for to be read:
Crying, 'Oh you cruel billows that washed my love on shore,
That I might behold his sweet features once more.'

THE HAND OF GLORY

THE fear of witchcraft dominated the lives of the people of the North Yorkshire Moors, until well into the last century. The parish of Danby possessed a gruesome object that struck fear and terror into the hearts of the dalesfolk. This was the Hand of Glory—a device which superstitious burglars considered an essential part of their kit until the early nineteenth century. This hand was discovered in an old cottage in the parish of Danby. When the new owner was undertaking some extensive alterations on the property, the relic was discovered on a great oak beam that was exposed when some of the old panelling was removed. This talisman of robbers and evil-doers may be read about in the *Ingoldsby Legends,* and a preserved example of one can be seen in all its ghoulish splendour in Whitby Museum.

Representations of the human hand have been used as charms long before the Christian era set in. Its use as a charm against enchantment can be traced back seven or eight hundred years before the birth of Christ. Models representing the hand have been believed in for the safeguarding of the home against magic and evil, and in some Christian churches even today care is taken to hold the fingers in certain positions during the benediction.

The hand was that of an executed criminal, cut off the body while the corpse was still hanging from the gibbet. For centuries, this grim and grisly object had been used by evil men for sinister and criminal purposes. The preparation of the object was quite simple—all you needed were a few ordinary everyday articles such as salt and pepper, saltpetre and candle wax, and of course the main ingredient—the hand of a gibbeted criminal. The blood was squeezed out of the hand, and the hand embalmed in a piece of shroud and steeped in a solution of saltpetre, salt and pepper for two weeks before being dried out in the sun. A candle was also an essential part of the proceedings. This was made from another number of curious ingredients such as hanged man's fat, wax and Lapland sesame. This candle was then fixed between the fingers of the hand and lit when the burglar broke into a house. Hypnotic and paralysing powers were attributed to the owner of this ghostly hand. It could immediately render a victim helpless and incapable of moving from the spot. If everything was done correctly it would also render the thief invisible, and unlock the doors. But all of this preparation was useless without recitation of the following incantation:

Let those who rest more deeply sleep;
Let those awake their vigils keep;
Oh, Hand of Glory shed thy light;
Direct us to our spoil tonight.

In Yorkshire during the eighteenth century it was not an uncommon practice for witches to engage in this degrading trade which was extremely profitable for them—hands fetching up to fifty pounds each. It was believed that the candle's spell could only be broken by putting out its flames with blood or skimmed milk—then the household would awake.

Sir Walter Scott in his novel *Antiquary* tells in detail of the supposed powers which lie in this Hand of Glory. He describes its preparation thus: 'The hand has to be wrapped in a cloth—part of a winding sheet—and squeezed of any blood in the veins, then put into an earthenware pot with pickling spices and salt-petre, until the hand is mummified. A candle has next to be made with pitch wax, the fat of a hanged man, 'virgin wax' and mustard oil. The dried shrivelled hand has to have this candle fixed in its fingers, and lighted: now the charm will work.' Strange tales centred around these fearsome hands have persisted, and accounts of their use have been found in many countries. Yorkshire not only possesses one of these rare relics, but also has the most authentic story concerning one of these hands.

High on Stainmore in the autumn of 1797, on the Bowes–Brough road stood an old coaching inn called *Spital Inn*, once owned by George Alderson. It was late in October on one cold stormy night and the family were sitting by the fire preparing to retire to bed. The few customers that they had had that night had long since gone. Suddenly a loud banging was heard and George sent the servant girl Bella to

open the door. Before her stood a bent old woman, dressed in a long cloak and hood hiding her features. She begged to be allowed to come in and rest a while. The old lady was invited in and made comfortable by the warm fire. George was unwilling to turn anyone out on such a night and offered her a place by the fire to spend the night. Presently the family went up to bed, leaving Bella alone with the old lady. For a while she tried to make polite conversation with the stranger, but only received a few curt replies in rather a low gruff voice. Then Bella noticed with surprise that when the stranger put out her leg in order to push a log further onto the fire, that 'she' was wearing heavy riding boots beneath the long skirts. Bella became very suspicious and was determined to keep an eye on the stranger. She lay down on the settle and pretended to go to sleep. When the stranger was suitably satisfied that Bella was asleep he threw back his hood and took from his cloak a shrunken, withered hand and placed a candle between the stiff bony fingers and lit it. Bella was frightened, but she kept very still while the man muttered his strange words of incantation. At once the flame of the candle grew to an intense, brilliant light. Immediately the man withdrew the heavy bolts on the large oak door, and put a whistle to his lips.

Suddenly Bella was on her feet and threw herself at the man sending him hurtling out into the dark. Before he could regain his feet the maid had turned the lock and bolted the door. She ran upstairs to her master's room shouting and banging on the door but there was no response. She went into the room and found them lying in a trance. After a few minutes of trying in vain to wake them, Bella ran downstairs to find the horrible hand was still burning brightly. She tried to blow it out, without success, so she picked up a bowl of milk and poured it over the terrifyingly eerie light. It went out at once, and the spell was immediately broken. George and his son, awakened from their heavy sleep came running downstairs with guns in their hands. George shouted to the gang outside to go away or he would shoot. When they refused his son fired in the direction of the voices. The robbers then shouted to George to give them their hand back, and then they would go away and leave them in peace. In reply to this the inn-keeper's son fired again and the robbers fled in panic. The next morning they found a pool of blood on the road and heard later that the whole gang had been caught. They were later tried and hanged. The Hand of Glory had been left behind and remained in George's possession for many years, probably as a reminder of the night when Bella's prompt actions had saved the family. A sixteenth century map described the place as 'the Spittle on Stainmore—the one inn for the entertainment of travellers'!

BEGGAR'S BRIDGE

THE River Esk drains the northern slopes of the Cleveland Hills which rise to a height of nearly 1,500 feet above sea-level. The river flows due east through a deep valley for the greater part of its course. Amidst overhanging trees Beggar's Bridge is to be found in the village of Glaisdale, nestling amongst some of the most beautiful scenery in the Esk valley. It is a beautiful narrow pack-horse bridge spanning the Esk with a single arch. This bridge was built early in the seventeenth century by Thomas Ferris and it was formerly known as Ferris Bridge. It bears his coat of arms and also the date 1619. The single segmental arch, with arch rings in two orders, has a total span of eighteen yards and the actual roadway is only six and a half feet wide.

There have been many stories and poems written about the bridge, and songs sung. These have been mostly concerned with the story of how the bridge got its name, but the following is a different love story:

At T' Beggar's Brig

by A. Stanley Umpleby

Jim:
T'skey's owerkessen, let's stan' o' t'brig
An' watch t'cloods reeace ahint yon rig;
Wa maun't gan far, t'wind's i' bad airt,
Wa's a'e sum muck afoor wa pairt.
Leeak at yon ring aroond t'awd meean,
Ther'll bi sum snaw or summat seean:
'Ark at t'awd ullots doon in t'wood,
An' Esk theer, tearin' by i' flood
That's t'music at Ah likes ti 'ear—
A moorland beck ootsahd t'back deear
If Ah'd 'ed that, sum wark an' thee,
They'd neean see me at Thornaby!

Jane:
Why Jim, thoo's nivver ax'd ma yit!
Let's finnd a spot wheer wa can sit.
Ah used ti think thoo liked Sal Raw—
Thoo 'appen diz for owt Ah knaw!
Sha allus reckons sha likes thee;
Diz thoo kiss 'er like thoo diz me?
'Cos if thoo diz, wa san't agree—
Thoo mun tak 'er ti Thornaby!

Jim:
Ah seear Ah deean't; Ah nivver 'ev;
Sha cums fre t'spot 'at Ah cum frev:
They lived gain and tiv us up t'Deeal.
Wa offens used ti reeace ti skeeal—
Reeace oot o' seeat o' ther lahl Cis—
An' then wa sumtahms 'ed a kiss,
Bud t'kisses warn't like Ah gies thee—
Noo, will tu gan ti Thornaby?

Jane:
Why noo, if what thoo sez is reet,
An' thoo can luv ma oot o' seet,
An' if thoo'll sweear Ahs'll gan.
But deean't let on yer ti your Keeate.
By gow, this 'ere's a wankly seeat!
Ah'll let 'er knaw 'at thee an' me
'll wed and live at Thornaby!

The story of how this bridge was built is well known locally. It concerns a young man by the name of Tom Ferris. He lived on the Egton side of the river, and on the Glaisdale side lived his sweetheart, a young lady from a well-to-do family—a charming lady whom he wanted to marry. The lady must indeed have been charming to have inspired in him such devotion as he showed, because in those days there was no bridge, and he had to wade across the River Esk to do his courting. No doubt the lady was very flattered by such dashing behaviour even though she had to content herself with a somewhat damp lover. For a long time the course of their love ran very far from smoothly as her father did not approve of the association because Tom had no money of his own. Because of this the couple had to meet secretly by the river. Tom could not ask for her hand in marriage because of his lack of money, and as there was none to be made in Glaisdale, he decided to go away to sea to make his fortune, while she was to wait faithfully for his return, no matter how long he might be. She was probably very confident that she would not have to wait too long, and guessed that a young man so resolute as her lover would go through the flames of hell for her sake. When they parted young Ferris knew that his lady would wait for him as faithfully as if they were already engaged. What he did or where he went no one knows for sure, and there is nothing to tell us. But since he was in a hurry to make good, and his motivation was high, one may assume that he probably went to work for a shipping company at Whitby—as fortunes were easy to come by at sea. There would be plenty of ships in Whitby ready to give a young adventurer of the right sort his chance.

In those days the shipping trade was a very lucrative one where silks and spices were brought to market with no questions asked. But whatever it was that Tom did while he was away, prosper he did, exceedingly, and it was not long before he came back with enough money in his pockets to make him a very suitable catch for any young lady. But there was only one lady for Tom and he returned with a faithful heart ready to part with all his riches. He was very eager to see his sweetheart, to tell her the good news, but he was to be disappointed because as he came back along his side of the river, he noticed that the Esk was in full flood. The turbulent waters roared with such ferocity that even a very strong swimmer would not have survived. And Tom, for all his devotion was not so stupid as to throw away his life for a little bravado. He was very upset and disappointed that he could not hold the girl he loved in his arms. They had to be content to shout greetings across the foaming depths of the Esk, from one bank to another. Eventually when the waters subsided, the two lovers were able to resume their courtship and he made his way to her in the fashion to which she was accustomed. They were soon married—the money having a definite soothing effect on her father. But Tom swore that no true lovers in Glaisdale would ever again be kept apart by a flood. So he devoted part of his new found wealth to building a bridge across the river. This beautiful bridge should have been called 'Lover's Bridge' in memory of the builder who was determined that no one should ever again be compelled to suffer the pain that he had endured. But the bridge became known as 'Beggar's Bridge' because they say that Ferris was little more than a beggar when he left to seek his fortune.

The Beggar's Bridge

by Mrs. George Davison

They talk of dales and hills in Wales,
As the loveliest in our isle;
But the Yorkshire dells and rocky fells,
Where the bright sun beams on the sparkling streams,
Are all forgot the while.

You may roam for hours 'mid sweet spring flowers,
With the gurgling 'beck' beneath,
While the rustling breeze just parts the trees,
And reveals the sweep of the wild woods deep,
Shut in the darkling hearth.

You may hear the note of the blackbird float,
From the top of each tall ash tree,
When he pours his song each evening long;
For in 'true love' tales such romantic dales,
Must needs abundant be.

The dalesmen say that their light archway
Is due to an Egton man,
Whose love was tried by a whelming tide;
I heard the tale in its native vale,
And thus the legend ran:

'Why lingers my lov'd one? Oh! Why does he roam
On the last winter's evening that hails him at home?
He promised to see me once more ere he went,
But the long rays of gloaming all lonely I've spent;
The stones at the fording no longer I see;
Ah! The darkness of night has concealed them from me.'

The maiden of Glaisdale sat lonely at eve,
And the cold stormy night saw her hopelessly grieve;
But when she looked forth from her casement at morn,
The maiden of Glaisdale was truly forlorn!
For the stones were engulfed where she looked for them last
By the deep swollen Esk that rolled rapidly past;
And vainly she strove with her tear-bedimmed eye,
The pathway she gazed on last night to descry.

Her lover had come to the brink of the tide,
And to stem its swift current repeatedly tried;
But the rough whirling eddy still swept him ashore,
And relentlessly bade him attempt it no more,
Exhausted he climbed the steep side of the brae,
And looked up the dale ere he turned him away;
Ah! From her far window a light flickered dim,
And he knew she was faithfully watching for him.

'I go to seek my fortune love,
In a far, far, distant land;
And without thy parting blessing, love
I am forced to quit the strand.

'But over Arncliffe's brow, my love,
I see thy twinkling light;
And when deeper waters part us, love
'Twill be my beacon bright.

'If fortune ever favour me,
St. Hilda! Hear my vow!
No lover again in my native plain,
Shall be thwarted as I am now.

One day I'll come to claim my bride,
As a worthy and wealthy man!
And my well earned gold shall raise a bridge
Across this torrent's span.'

The rover came back from a far distant land,
And he claimed of the maid her long-promised hand;
But he built, ere he won her, the bridge of his vow,
And the lovers of Egton pass over it now.

THE MOORLAND CROSSES

THE stone crosses of north Yorkshire mostly date back to Saxon times, 'From the dawn of Christianity the cross has been the symbol of our belief.' The cross was first the sign by which the Christians recognised each other in times of persecution and danger. The erection of crosses became quite common very shortly after the introduction of Christianity amongst the Anglo-Saxons. They were without doubt erected in the first place as a deterrent to evil spirits and as a reminder of the holy religion.

Crosses were also erected to commemorate great victories or memorable events, and as resting places where the funeral processions of important persons rested on their way to be buried, so that passers-by might think to say a prayer for the departed soul. Crosses were frequently erected where four roads met and at the entrance to a village or at the centre of a village. They also marked the site of a murder or a sudden death, or were used as guide posts, and to denote the division of parishes.

Moorland crosses (top, left to right): Whitby Abbey Cross; Fat Betty or White Cross. Bottom: Ralph's Cross; Lilla Cross.

The most familiar of the moorland crosses is the Whitby Abbey Cross, but the origin of this cross is uncertain. Further over the moors stands Lilla Cross. It can be found by a well-marked track from Ellerbeck just past Fylingdales Early Warning Station. This cross is possibly the oldest in the area and is mentioned in the earliest charters giving the boundaries of Whitby Strand. It is positioned at the highest point for miles and marks the apex of the Abbey lands where the lordships of Whitby, Sneaton and the Duchy of Lancaster meet. Lilla Cross is also on the road from Whitby to Hackness where Hilda had a retreat, and no doubt often went. Lilla Cross was erected about 626 A.D. to commemorate the death of Lilla, an officer of the court of Edwin, King of Northumbria, who died saving the life of the king from an assassination attempt at the sacrifice of his own life.

For the more energetic a walk on to the moors from Danby leads to Fat Betty, Ralph's Cross and Old Ralph's Cross. Ralph's Cross is close to the roadside leading from Castleton to Rosedale. Old Ralph's Cross is about 400 yards to the west from Ralph's Cross, and Fat Betty/White Cross stands a similar distance from Ralph's Cross in an easterly direction. These three stone crosses stand in an almost straight line, all within a distance of not more than half a mile. Ralph's Cross is about seven feet in height and marks the spot where a poor traveller died of hunger and exposure. His death had quite an impact on a certain farmer called Ralph so that he erected a cross where the body was found and at the top of the cross was a hollow where it was the custom for those wealhier than this poor traveller to place any coins they could spare, thereby being a means of saving other poor travellers from such a fate. Old Ralph's Cross marks the place where two groups of lost travellers found one another and safety and Fat Betty is a boundary stone. This very bulky, rough hewn square stone forms the corner boundary stone where three lines of boundary posts all meet, marking the point where the moors of Danby, Westerdale and Rosedale converge.

WEDDING CUSTOMS

THERE were many traditional customs carried out at weddings in this area. Most are no longer practised, but once it was customary that as the bridal party left the church gate, and throughout their walk to the bride's home, they were often met by friends carrying hot pots of steaming punch or sweet and spiced ale, and were offered drinks from all the houses on the route from the church to the reception. Most of the villagers were guests as well as relations, and after the service and reception, the wedding guests would all congregate in a field not too far away from the pub. Here foot races would be held with small prizes for the winners. And then everyone would retire to the pub where a collection was held to pay for the drinks. A popular song sung in the pubs on the occasions of these wedding parties was the following:

The bride's good health is now beginning
In spite of the Turk or the Spanish King
The groom's good health we'll not let pass
We'll have them both into one glass
See See See that he drinks it all
See See See that he lets none fall
For if he does he shall have two
And so shall the company all.

Another common custom at weddings was the race for the bride's garter. The male guests usually started from the church door as soon as the ring was placed on the bride's finger and they had to run to the bride's door. The winner of this race claimed the privilege of removing the garter from the bride's leg. This garter was highly valued as it was considered to be a potent love charm—that is assuming that the new husband was not of the jealous kind!